HABITAT FRAGMENTATION AND ITS IMPACT ON MALAYAN TIGER POPULATIONS

Habitat Fragmentation and its Impact on Malayan Tiger Populations

Ehsan Sheroy

Spectra Enterprise

CONTENTS

INDEX

INTRODUCTION

In the thick rainforests and rambling scenes of the Malay Promontory, the tricky Malayan tiger (Panthera tigris jacksoni) when wandered as a dominant hunter, encapsulating the wild pith of Southeast Asia. Nonetheless, the mind boggling embroidery of this regular shelter is unwinding, destroyed by a quiet however inescapable power — environment discontinuity. This acquaintance sets out on an excursion with disentangle the complex ramifications of environment fracture on Malayan tiger populaces, investigating the natural complexities, the social meaning of these huge felines, and the critical requirement for protection methodologies to safeguard an animal varieties near the precarious edge of hazard.

**1. The Malayan Tiger: A Symbol of Southeast Asian Biodiversity:

The Malayan tiger, a subspecies of the Indochinese tiger, holds a one of a kind spot in the rich biodiversity of the Malay Promontory. Famous for its unmistakable profound orange coat and limited dark stripes, this catlike seal has for quite some time been interlaced with the social legacy of the district. Adored in legends and craftsmanship, the Malayan tiger represents strength, flexibility, and the untamed soul of nature.

**2. The Delicate Biological systems of the Malay Landmass:

The lavish rainforests, mangrove swamps, and various environments of the Malay Landmass have filled in as the regular territory for the Malayan tiger for quite a long time. These scenes, when adjacent and extensive, gave an optimal setting to these dominant hunters to flourish. Be that as it may, the fast change of the locale because of human exercises has started a fountain of biological changes, prompting the discontinuity of these once-continuous territories.

**3. Characterizing Environment Fracture: A Secretive Danger to Biodiversity:

Environment fracture, a term that could appear to be harmless, covers an intense danger to the sensitive equilibrium of biological systems. It alludes to the interaction by which enormous, nonstop environments are separated into more modest, secluded sections, frequently because of human exercises like urbanization, agribusiness, and framework advancement. This fracture changes the spatial design of environments, upsetting the interconnected snare of life and presenting extreme difficulties to species that depend on broad regions.

**4. The Human Impression: Urbanization, Horticulture, and Foundation Advancement:

The determined extension of human exercises has left a permanent impression on the scenes that once supported the Malayan tiger. Urbanization, driven by populace development and financial turn of events, changes immense lots of wild into substantial wildernesses. Farming practices, while giving food, infringe upon regular living spaces. The development of streets, interstates, and other framework projects further analyzes the tiger's area, confining populaces and restricting their capacity to uninhibitedly wander.

**5. Environmental Implications of Territory Fracture:

The outcomes of living space fracture stretch out a long ways past the noticeable change of scenes. For the Malayan tiger, an animal groups that requires broad domains to chase, mate, and lay out regions, divided territories force impossible difficulties. Diminished admittance to prey, upset mating designs, and expanded weakness to poaching are among the environmental repercussions that compromise the actual endurance of these grand animals.

**6. Confinement and Hereditary Variety: A Hereditary Implosion:

One of the significant effects of environment fracture is the separation of tiger populaces, prompting a dangerous decrease in hereditary variety. In divided scenes, the open doors for tigers to connect and raise across various gatherings decrease fundamentally. The subsequent hereditary segregation builds the gamble of inbreeding as well as uplifts weakness to illnesses and lessens the versatile limit of the populace.

**7. The Risky Street to Annihilation: Populace Decline and Inbreeding Despondency:

As divided living spaces limit tiger populaces to more modest regions, the unavoidable result is a decrease in generally speaking populace numbers. Inbreeding discouragement, a peculiarity where the posterity of firmly related people experience the ill effects of decreased wellness and wellbeing, arises as a quiet yet deadly danger. The Malayan tiger, previously confronting the tensions of natural surroundings misfortune, presently wrestles with the ghost of a hereditary bottleneck that could push it unsafely near eradication.

**8. Human-Untamed life Struggle: A Result of Broken Limits:

The infringement of human exercises into tiger domains achieves an unwanted outcome — human-untamed life struggle. As divided environments force tigers into closer vicinity to human settlements, clashes emerge over shared assets.

Domesticated animals plunder, dangers to human security, and retaliatory killings become familiar indications of this contention, intensifying the difficulties looked by Malayan tiger populaces.

**9. Social and Emblematic Significance: Tigers in Fantasy and Reality:

Past their natural importance, Malayan tigers hold a profound social and representative significance in the hearts of individuals of the Malay Promontory. In native convictions and fables, tigers are many times loved as legendary creatures, encapsulating both trepidation and regard. The social texture that meshes tigers into the stories of networks highlights the characteristic association between human social orders and the regular world.

**10. Preservation Goals: Diagramming a Course for the Malayan Tiger's Endurance:

Notwithstanding territory discontinuity and its inescapable effect, the basic for preservation endeavors becomes critical. Safeguarding the Malayan tiger requires a multi-layered approach that tends to the biological difficulties as well as the financial variables adding to natural surroundings corruption. Moderates, policymakers, and nearby networks should join in a coordinated work to get the fate of this notorious species.

**11. Reestablishing Availability: Hallways and Scene Level Preparation:

Turning around the impacts of territory fracture requires the rebuilding of availability between detached tiger populaces. Natural life passageways, decisively arranged and safeguarded pathways that take into account the development of creatures between divided territories, arise as pivotal parts of preservation techniques. Scene level preparation, integrating natural network, turns into a foundation for guaranteeing the endurance of the Malayan tiger.

**12. Local area Commitment and Supportable Practices: A Common Obligation:

The way to preservation achievement entwines with the dynamic contribution of neighborhood networks. Engaging people group to become stewards of tiger territories includes cultivating mindfulness, advancing reasonable land use rehearses, and giving monetary motivators to preservation. At the point when networks embrace their job as caretakers of the land, the possibilities for conjunction and economical living space the board light up.

**13. Worldwide Cooperation: A Worldwide Obligation to Save the Malayan Tiger:

The preservation of the Malayan tiger rises above public limits. Worldwide cooperation, including adjoining nations, protection associations, and the worldwide local area, becomes central. Shared research, information trade, and composed protection endeavors add to a brought together front against the powers of territory discontinuity that undermine the Malayan tiger.

1. Brief overview of the Malayan tiger

   Settled inside the lavish rainforests and spellbinding scenes of the Malay Landmass, the Malayan tiger (Panthera tigris jacksoni) remains as an image of both the locale's rich biodiversity and the difficulties looked by its lead species. As a particular subspecies of the Indochinese tiger, the Malayan tiger charms with its interesting elements, social importance, and the tricky status that highlights the dire requirement for protection endeavors. In this outline, we unwind the enamoring story of the Malayan tiger, investigating its actual qualities, territory, social characteristics, and the perplexing snare of elements that compromise its presence.

   **1. Actual Qualities: A Striking Presence in the Wilderness:

   The Malayan tiger's appearance is described by a blend of class and strength. Eminent for its profound orange to rosy gold fur, the tiger's jacket is embellished with thin dark stripes that act as both disguise in the thick vegetation and an unmistakable marker of individual character. Its underparts, including the gut and the internal side of the appendages, are commonly white, and a few people might display varieties in coat hue.

   The Malayan tiger is known for its vigorous form, with strong appendages and an advanced body. Grown-up guys for the most part weigh between 220 to 300 pounds, while females are marginally more modest, making an appearance the scope of 150 to 220 pounds. These actual properties are fundamental transformations for a hunter that explores the difficult landscape of the Malaysian rainforests, where dexterity and strength are critical for endurance.

   **2. Territory: Rainforests and Then some:

   The regular environment of the Malayan tiger traverses the different biological systems of the Malay Promontory, enveloping essential and auxiliary rainforests, mangrove marshes, and even prairies. This large number of territories mirrors the flexibility of the Malayan tiger, permitting it to flourish in different scenes. In any case, its essential fortress stays the thick and biodiverse rainforests that give more than adequate cover to following prey and laying out domains. These natural surroundings, once bordering and far reaching, are currently progressively divided because of human exercises, introducing a basic test to the Malayan tiger's endurance.

Urbanization, rural extension, and framework advancement have cut up the once-ceaseless scenes, detaching tiger populaces and restricting their capacity to uninhibitedly meander.

**3. Social Characteristics: Single and Regional Hunters:

The Malayan tiger is dominatingly a single and regional hunter, known for its ability in exploring the thick vegetation of its living space. Every grown-up tiger lays out and wildly safeguards a domain, stamping it with fragrance markings and vocalizations to prevent interlopers. These regions, pivotal for hunting and mating, can traverse immense regions, mirroring the requirement for far reaching scenes to help individual tigers.

Tigers are crepuscular trackers, meaning they are generally dynamic during first light and nightfall. Their sharp feelings of sight and hearing, combined with their solidarity and dexterity, make them exceptionally proficient hunters. Malayan tigers go after various ungulates, including deer and wild hog, adjusting their hunting procedures to the accessibility of prey in their particular environments.

**4. Multiplication and Life Cycle: Guaranteeing the Continuation of the Species:

The conceptive pattern of the Malayan tiger is intently attached to its regional way of behaving. Female tigers come into estrus generally every three to about a month, flagging their status to mate. Mating matches take part in romance customs, and after a growth time of around 93 to 112 days, a female brings forth a litter of whelps. The quantity of whelps can go from two to four, and the mother assumes on the sole liability of raising and safeguarding them.

Offspring are conceived visually impaired and helpless, depending on their mom for sustenance and security. As they develop, the mother bestows significant hunting and basic instincts to her posterity. The whelps commonly stay with their mom until they are around 18 to two years old, after which they steadily spread to lay out their regions. This dispersal is a basic stage in keeping up with hereditary variety inside tiger populaces.

**5. Social Importance: Tigers in Folklore and Old stories:

The Malayan tiger holds an extraordinary spot in the social legacy of the Malay Promontory. Respected as an image of solidarity, mental fortitude, and power, tigers highlight unmistakably in neighborhood folklore and fables. Stories portray tigers as enchanted creatures, frequently connected with defensive spirits or as heroes in stories that convey moral examples. The representative meaning of the Malayan tiger is profoundly implanted in the practices and stories of the native networks of the area.

Creative portrayals, from customary canvases to current social articulations, regularly highlight the Malayan tiger as an intense image. Its picture is embellished on banners, utilized as a mascot for sports groups, and fills in as a wellspring of motivation for different types of creative articulation. This social importance highlights the inborn association between the Malayan tiger and the personality of the networks that offer its living space.

**6. Dangers to Endurance: The Shadow of Territory Discontinuity:

Notwithstanding its venerated status, the Malayan tiger faces a risky future, principally because of the constant infringement of human exercises on its environment. Living space discontinuity arises as a basic danger, disturbing the regular scenes that are fundamental for the tiger's endurance. The once-continuous hallways that permitted tigers to meander uninhibitedly have been analyzed by streets, metropolitan regions, and rural breadths, prompting disengagement and decreased admittance to prey.

Human-untamed life struggle adds one more layer of intricacy to the difficulties looked by Malayan tigers. As their regions cross-over with human settlements, clashes emerge over shared assets, prompting retaliatory killings and further imperiling these grand hunters.

**7. Preservation Endeavors: Graphing a Way to Endurance:

Perceiving the dire need to moderate the Malayan tiger, devoted endeavors are in progress to address the complex difficulties it faces. Preservation drives incorporate a range of techniques, going from living space reclamation and insurance to local area commitment and worldwide cooperation.

The foundation of untamed life hallways and the safeguarding of basic living spaces are fundamental parts of these endeavors. Moderates work to bring issues to light about the significance of conjunction, alleviating human-natural life struggle through imaginative arrangements, for example, early advance notice frameworks and local area based enemy of poaching drives.

Worldwide cooperation, including states, preservation associations, and the worldwide local area, becomes basic in shielding the fate of the Malayan tiger. Shared research, information trade, and facilitated preservation procedures add to a unified front against the powers that compromise the endurance of this famous species.

2. Significance of Malayan tigers in the ecosystem

The Malayan tiger (Panthera tigris jacksoni) is something other than a notorious image; it assumes a crucial part in the fragile embroidery of the Southeast Asian biological system, impacting the equilibrium and wellbeing of its territories in significant ways.

As dominant hunters, Malayan tigers apply hierarchical guideline, molding the overflow and conduct of prey species, and adding to the general biodiversity and flexibility of their environments.

**1. Directing Prey Populaces:

At the head of the pecking order, Malayan tigers go about as controllers of prey populaces, forestalling the overpopulation of herbivores that could somehow or another corrupt vegetation and disturb the environmental equilibrium. Through their predation on ungulates like deer and wild hog, tigers assist with keeping up with the wellbeing and variety of plant networks, by implication helping a heap of different animal types subject to these biological systems.

**2. Keeping up with Biodiversity:

Tigers are cornerstone species, meaning their presence is excessively persuasive in keeping up with the construction and capability of their environments. By controlling the overflow of specific species, they make conditions that permit a more prominent variety of plant and creature life to flourish. The deficiency of tigers could set off a fountain of biological irregular characteristics, possibly prompting the decay or eradication of different species inside a similar environment.

**3. Saving Natural surroundings Respectability:

The hunting and regional ways of behaving of Malayan tigers add to the protection of natural surroundings respectability. Tigers require tremendous regions for their exercises, and in doing as such, they assist with keeping up with the availability and usefulness of biological systems. The foundation of domains includes aroma checking and vocalizations, which, thus, adds to the making of distinct spaces where biodiversity can thrive.

**4. Improving Hereditary Variety:

Tigers assume a significant part in upgrading hereditary variety inside their populaces. Their boundless domains work with quality stream between people, forestalling the pessimistic impacts of inbreeding. This hereditary variety is fundamental for the drawn out versatility and flexibility of the species, guaranteeing their capacity to adapt to natural changes and dangers.

**5. Seed Dispersal:

Tigers accidentally add to seed dispersal as they travel through their regions. Seeds from consumed natural products are saved in various areas through the tiger's scat, supporting the recovery of plant species.

This circuitous job in seed dispersal further concretes their importance in the recovery and variety of vegetation inside their environments.

**6. Marks of Biological system Wellbeing:

The presence and conduct of Malayan tigers act as significant marks of the general strength of their biological systems. Their populace elements, regenerative achievement, and state of being mirror the prosperity of the natural surroundings they possess. Checking these markers gives significant experiences into the more extensive soundness of the environment, assisting protectionists with surveying the effect of human exercises and environmental change.

**7. Social and Ecotourism Worth:

Past their environmental job, Malayan tigers hold tremendous social importance in the locale. Their presence in the wild is a wellspring of pride and respect for neighborhood networks, adding to the social character of the Malay Landmass. Furthermore, tigers draw in ecotourism, giving financial motivating forces to nearby networks and adding to the preservation of their living spaces.

In synopsis, the Malayan tiger is a cornerstone animal types whose importance resonates all through the complex snare of life in Southeast Asian environments. Their part in directing prey populaces, keeping up with biodiversity, protecting environment honesty, improving hereditary variety, supporting seed dispersal, and filling in as marks of biological system wellbeing highlights the indispensable worth of these great enormous felines. Perceiving and protecting their spot in the biological system isn't simply a natural basic yet a promise to the rich biodiversity and social legacy of the Malay Promontory.

3. Introduction to habitat fragmentation as a critical issue

In the many-sided embroidery of the normal world, territories once consistently woven together are currently disentangling, leading to an unavoidable and basic issue known as territory fracture. This peculiarity, driven transcendently by human exercises, represents a significant danger to biodiversity, environment flexibility, and the sensitive equilibrium that supports life on The planet. As we dive into the intricacies of environment discontinuity, it becomes clear that its repercussions stretch out a long ways past the noticeable modification of scenes — a major test requires critical consideration and deliberate endeavors for moderation.

**1. Characterizing Environment Discontinuity: A Disturbance in the Normal Request:

Living space discontinuity alludes to the interaction by which enormous, persistent environments are divided into more modest, disengaged patches, frequently as an outcome of human exercises. This adjustment of scenes upsets the spatial course of action of biological systems, presenting hindrances that obstruct the development of species, modify natural cycles, and at last change the actual texture of the climate. The results of environment discontinuity are sweeping and multi-layered, influencing both verdure across different biological systems all around the world.

**2. Human Impression: The Impetus for Interruption:

The essential driver behind environment fracture is the growing impression of human exercises. Quick urbanization, horticultural extension, foundation improvement, and asset extraction have made a permanent imprint on the regular world. As human populaces develop and economies advance, the interest for land escalates, prompting the change of once-perfect natural surroundings into divided patches, confined in the midst of an ocean of anthropogenic scenes. The human impression turns into the impetus for the disentangling of environments, making a heap of difficulties for the species that depend on coterminous living spaces for their endurance.

**3. Natural Results: A Far reaching influence through Environments:

The natural results of environment discontinuity are likened to an expanding influence, pervading through the interconnected snare of life. For some species, the capacity to move uninhibitedly across scenes is fundamental for scavenging, reproducing, and keeping up with hereditary variety. Divided living spaces upset these crucial exercises, prompting diminished admittance to assets, disconnection of populaces, and an expanded weakness to outside dangers like predation and sickness.

**4. Hereditary Disconnection: The Quiet Danger to Biodiversity:

One of the most slippery results of natural surroundings fracture is hereditary disconnection. As populaces become restricted to more modest, detached patches, open doors for interbreeding lessen. The subsequent hereditary segregation can prompt inbreeding misery, diminished wellness, and an expanded helplessness to infections. After some time, this hereditary bottleneck undermines the versatility and long haul endurance of species, further worsening the biodiversity emergency.

**5. Influence on Cornerstone Species: Unwinding the Trap of Association:

Cornerstone species, which assume lopsidedly powerful parts in keeping up with environment design and capability, are especially helpless against natural surroundings fracture.

Their reduced presence or adjusted conduct can set off flowing impacts, upsetting the complicated trap of reliance inside biological systems. This can prompt a decrease in biodiversity, an expansion in obtrusive species, and the destabilization of environmental cycles that are key to the strength of whole biological systems.

**6. Expanded Human-Untamed life Struggle: A Result of Broken Limits:

As regular scenes capitulate to fracture, untamed life ends up in nearer vicinity to human settlements. This elevated connection makes way for expanded human-untamed life struggle, where creatures adventure into human-ruled regions looking for assets. Animals plunder, dangers to human wellbeing, and retaliatory killings become familiar indications of this contention, further heightening the difficulties looked by both untamed life and human networks.

**7. Monetary Effects: A Burden on Biological system Administrations:

The monetary effects of living space discontinuity are not restricted to the domain of biodiversity alone. Biological system administrations, including fertilization, water cleaning, and environment guideline, are compromised as living spaces section and debase. The deficiency of these administrations not just influences the prosperity of normal environments yet additionally puts extra weights on human social orders that depend on these administrations for agribusiness, water supply, and environment versatility.

**8. Worldwide Ramifications: A Common Test for Humankind:

Living space discontinuity is definitely not a restricted issue; its suggestions reverberate internationally. The deficiency of biodiversity, disturbances to biological system administrations, and the fuel of environmental change are difficulties that rise above borders. As natural surroundings part and species face expanding dangers, the perplexing interaction of environmental frameworks is compromised, with repercussions that broaden well past the quick areas of human intercession.

In the parts that follow, we leave on a complete investigation of environment discontinuity, looking at its causes, outcomes, and the basic job it plays in the destiny of explicit species, biological systems, and at last, the eventual fate of our planet. From the littlest organic entities to the biggest hunters, no component of the regular world is immaculate by the strings of territory fracture, making it an earnest and basic issue that requests our aggregate consideration and purposeful activity.

CHAPTER 1

Malayan Tiger Ecology And Behavior

The Malayan tiger (Panthera tigris jacksoni) remains as a charming image of the lively biological systems tracked down in the Malay Landmass and southern Thailand. This subtle large feline, recognized by its strikingly rich orange coat and strong dark stripes, involves a novel biological specialty. Understanding the complexities of Malayan tiger nature and conduct is fundamental for contriving powerful protection procedures and guaranteeing the endurance of this jeopardized species.

Territory Inclinations and Dispersion

Malayan tigers overwhelmingly possess the lavish and various tropical rainforests, evergreen backwoods, and mangrove bogs of the Malay Promontory. Their dispersion reaches out into the southern locales of Thailand, where the scene offers a blend of thick wildernesses and rough territories. These territories furnish the Malayan tiger with the best blend of cover, prey, and water sources fundamental for their endurance.

Not at all like some other tiger subspecies, Malayan tigers have adjusted to living in districts with high precipitation. The thick vegetation offers more than adequate cover for following prey and raising fledglings, making it an ideal climate for these slippery hunters. Also, the accessibility of water is essential, and the Malayan tiger is known to possess regions close to waterways and streams.

Job of Unblemished Woods in Supporting Tiger Populaces

The honesty of perfect timberlands assumes a fundamental part in supporting Malayan tiger populaces. Undisturbed environments give an abundance of assets, including a different cluster of prey species and adequate space for tigers to lay out regions. Enormous regions are fundamental for individual tigers to meet their dietary necessities and track down appropriate mates.

The unblemished biological systems of immaculate timberlands support a sensitive harmony among hunters and prey, guaranteeing a characteristic guideline of herbivore populaces. This equilibrium is pivotal for keeping up with the general soundness of the environment and forestalling overgrazing or consumption of plant species. The Malayan tiger, as a dominant hunter, is a cornerstone animal categories that manages the fragile balance of its natural surroundings.

Outline of Malayan Tiger Conduct and Propagation

Malayan tigers display a scope of ways of behaving that mirror their versatility and strength right at home. Single ordinarily, these tigers lay out regions to guarantee admittance to assets and to stay away from clashes with others. The size of a tiger's region relies upon variables, for example, the accessibility of prey, water sources, and the thickness of different tigers nearby.

Tigers are profoundly regional and use aroma stamping, vocalizations, and visual signs to impart their presence and lay out limits. The fragrance markings, frequently left on trees or shakes, act as an advance notice to different tigers to remain away. Vocalizations, including thunders and chuffing sounds, are utilized for significant distance correspondence and are especially significant during the mating season.

The conceptive way of behaving of Malayan tigers is a captivating part of their biology. Female tigers normally come into estrus for a concise period, flagging their status to mate. During this time, they leave aroma checks and express to draw in likely mates. Male tigers answer by watching their regions and effectively searching out females in estrus.

Mating matches take part in romance ceremonies, which might include common preparing, cuddling, and vocal associations. The growth time frame endures roughly 93-112 days, after which the female brings forth a litter of normally 2-4 whelps. The offspring are conceived visually impaired and helpless, depending totally on their mom for assurance and sustenance.

The maternal impulses of female Malayan tigers are striking. They make stowed away sanctums in thick vegetation to protect their whelps from likely dangers. The mother puts impressive time and exertion in sustaining and showing her whelps fundamental abilities to survive, including hunting methods, until they become free at something like year and a half old enough.

Difficulties to Malayan Tiger Environment and Conduct

In spite of the intrinsic versatility of Malayan tigers, their nature and conduct face various difficulties, fundamentally determined by human exercises. The main danger is environment misfortune because of deforestation, farming extension, and framework advancement. As immaculate timberlands are divided and lessened, the domains accessible for Malayan tigers contract, prompting expanded rivalry for assets and higher powerlessness to inbreeding.

The fracture of living spaces additionally disturbs the regular ways of behaving and development examples of Malayan tigers. Confined domains can bring about expanded clashes between people, prompting wounds or even fatalities.

Furthermore, the nearness of tigers to human settlements raises the probability of human-untamed life clashes, with tigers going after animals or, in outrageous cases, representing a danger to human security.

Another basic test is the unlawful natural life exchange, driven by the interest for tiger parts in conventional medication and extravagance merchandise. Poaching represents an immediate danger to Malayan tiger populaces, as their body parts are exceptionally desired. This unlawful exchange further mixtures the difficulties looked by these glorious felines, driving them nearer to the edge of annihilation.

Protection Endeavors: Adjusting Human Requirements and Tiger Endurance

Endeavors to ration Malayan tigers and their extraordinary nature are complex, requiring a blend of environment insurance, hostile to poaching measures, and local area commitment. The foundation of safeguarded regions and natural life halls is pivotal for keeping up with and reestablishing appropriate living spaces for tigers. These hallways work with the development of people between divided patches of backwoods, relieving the pessimistic impacts of environment discontinuity.

Preservation associations team up with state run administrations and nearby networks to execute hostile to poaching measures and implement regulations against untamed life dealing. The contribution of neighborhood networks is especially imperative, as their help can assist with guaranteeing the achievement and manageability of preservation drives. Schooling programs that bring issues to light about the significance of Malayan tigers in keeping up with solid environments and the possible outcomes of their eradication are fundamental parts of these endeavors.

Mechanical Arrangements and Developments in Tiger Protection

Progressions in innovation have shown to be significant devices in the preservation stockpile for Malayan tigers. Geographic Data Framework (GIS) and remote detecting advancements empower specialists to guide and screen tiger environments, distinguish possible dangers, and track changes in land use. Camera traps outfitted with movement sensors give pivotal information on tiger populaces, conduct, and development designs in remote and testing landscapes.

Cooperative endeavors between specialists, non-legislative associations (NGOs), and states influence innovation to improve the adequacy of protection methodologies. The utilization of information driven approaches works with proof based direction, guaranteeing that restricted assets are designated proficiently to resolve the most major problems confronting Malayan tiger populaces.

The Job of Global Cooperation in Tiger Preservation

Given the transboundary idea of the territories involved by Malayan tigers, global cooperation is vital for their protection. Nations sharing tiger populaces should organize endeavors to lay out and keep up with natural life passages, trade data on poaching exercises, and altogether address the more extensive difficulties of living space misfortune and debasement.

Worldwide associations, for example, the World Natural life Asset (WWF) and the Worldwide Tiger Gathering, assume an essential part in working with cooperation and diverting assets toward complete protection drives. The sharing of best practices, skill, and assets improves the general effect of preservation measures, cultivating an aggregate obligation to shielding the fate of Malayan tigers.

1.1 Habitat preferences and distribution

The Malayan tiger (Panthera tigris jacksoni) remains as a significant figure in the rich scenes of the Malay Promontory and southern Thailand. Understanding the multifaceted dance between the Malayan tiger and its environment is central for concocting powerful protection procedures and guaranteeing the proceeded with presence of this basically jeopardized subspecies.

Variation to Assorted Territories

Malayan tigers have shown an uncommon capacity to adjust to different territories inside their reach. While they are generally connected with tropical rainforests, their dispersion stretches out to a mosaic of biological systems, including evergreen backwoods, mangrove bogs, and optional timberlands. This versatility highlights the flexibility of the Malayan tiger notwithstanding environmental variety.

One of the characterizing elements of Malayan tigers is their variation to districts with high precipitation. Not at all like some other tiger subspecies, they have advanced to flourish in conditions with thick vegetation and bountiful water sources. This extraordinary variation is a demonstration of the animal categories' adaptability and capacity to possess different specialties inside the more extensive biological system.

Essential Natural surroundings: Tropical Rainforests

Tropical rainforests address the essential and favored natural surroundings for Malayan tigers. These rich and biodiverse biological systems give an ideal mix of variables pivotal for the endurance of the species. The thick overhang offers adequate cover for following prey, while the changed geography sets out open doors for vital hunting and regional foundation.

Inside the rainforest, Malayan tigers lay out regions that act as their selective spaces for hunting, mating, and raising posterity. The domains are painstakingly decided to enhance admittance to distinct advantages, for example, prey, water sources, and appropriate sanctum locales. The immense breadth of the rainforest takes into consideration the foundation of generally huge domains, fundamental for meeting the dietary requirements of individual tigers.

Evergreen Timberlands: An Optional Environment

Past tropical rainforests, Malayan tigers are known to occupy evergreen timberlands, described by a different cluster of widely varied vegetation. These living spaces share likenesses with rainforests yet may have somewhat unique vegetation designs and occasional varieties. Evergreen timberlands give an elective scene to the Malayan tiger to explore, guaranteeing a level of versatility notwithstanding changing natural circumstances.

In these conditions, tigers keep on showing their ability as dominant hunters, going after various herbivores that occupy these lavish environments. The versatility to evergreen backwoods exhibits the species' capacity to take advantage of various environmental specialties, adding to its endurance in different scenes.

Mangrove Marshes: A Novel Specialty

A fascinating feature of Malayan tiger biology is their presence in mangrove swamps, featuring their ability to flourish in conditions that could appear to be unwelcoming to other enormous feline species. Mangrove swamps are portrayed by saline water, flowing vacillations, and a novel mix of earthbound and sea-going environments. In these difficult natural surroundings, Malayan tigers exhibit their versatility by hunting various prey, including fish and other sea-going species.

The capacity to occupy mangrove swamps delineates the Malayan tiger's flexibility and the significance of rationing a scope of living spaces to guarantee the subspecies' drawn out endurance. Mangrove biological systems, frequently exposed to anthropogenic tensions, are basic for keeping up with biodiversity, and the presence of Malayan tigers highlights their job as cornerstone species in such conditions.

Appropriation Across the Malay Landmass and Southern Thailand

The appropriation of Malayan tigers is unpredictably attached to the geology of the Malay Landmass and southern Thailand. By and large, their reach covered a greater region, however living space misfortune and discontinuity have prompted a constriction of their conveyance. Today, Malayan tigers are principally tracked down in disengaged pockets of reasonable living space inside their reach.

The Malay Landmass, portrayed by a different scope of biological systems, fills in as the fortification for Malayan tigers. The coterminous scenes of essential and optional woods, combined with the presence of water bodies, give a helpful climate to the subspecies. Furthermore, the southern districts of Thailand offer comparative territories, taking into consideration the extension of their circulation across worldwide lines.

Difficulties to Dissemination: Territory Misfortune and Fracture

In spite of the flexibility of Malayan tigers to different natural surroundings, their circulation faces extreme difficulties principally determined by human exercises. Environment misfortune because of deforestation, agrarian extension, and foundation advancement has prompted the discontinuity of once-bordering scenes. This fracture represents an immediate danger to the dispersion examples of Malayan tigers, confining their developments and disconnecting populaces.

As unblemished timberlands give way to human-ruled scenes, the accessibility of appropriate natural surroundings reduces, and tigers are constrained into more modest, detached patches. These disconnected populaces face expanded dangers of inbreeding, hereditary inconsistencies, and a diminished capacity to adjust to changing natural circumstances. The outcomes of living space misfortune and discontinuity stretch out past the prompt effect on the appropriation of Malayan tigers; they echo through the whole environment, influencing biodiversity and natural security.

Preservation Basic: Safeguarding and Reestablishing Environments

Saving the conveyance of Malayan tigers requires a complete and purposeful preservation approach. Endeavors should zero in on safeguarding existing environments, reestablishing debased scenes, and laying out untamed life passages to reconnect divided regions. Safeguarded regions and stores assume an essential part in shielding the center territories that are crucial for the endurance and circulation of Malayan tigers.

Natural life halls are fundamental for keeping up with network between disconnected tiger populaces. These passages take into account the development of people, working with hereditary trade and decreasing the pessimistic impacts of inbreeding. Laying out and keeping up with these passages require joint effort between preservation associations, states, and neighborhood networks to guarantee the consistent progression of hereditary variety across scenes.

Human-Natural life Struggle Relief

Tending to human-natural life clashes is one more basic part of guaranteeing the feasible appropriation of Malayan tigers. As tigers' natural surroundings become progressively divided, their closeness to human settlements rises, prompting clashes over assets and wellbeing concerns.

Powerful relief systems include local area commitment, schooling, and the improvement of supportable practices that consider concurrence among tigers and nearby networks.

Adjusting Preservation and Improvement: A Fragile Condition

The test of moderating the appropriation of Malayan tigers is additionally muddled by the requirement for adjusted improvement. The developing human populace and the related interest for assets frequently lead to land-use changes that infringe upon tiger environments. Finding some kind of harmony among preservation and improvement requires inventive methodologies, manageable land-use arranging, and an acknowledgment of the characteristic worth of unblemished biological systems.

1.2 Role of pristine forests in sustaining tiger populations

Unblemished woods stand as the quiet watchmen of biodiversity, and for the Malayan tiger (Panthera tigris jacksoni), these undisturbed scenes are indispensable to its endurance. The unpredictable dance between Malayan tigers and unblemished timberlands incorporates regional elements, prey accessibility, and the safeguarding of hereditary variety. In understanding the significant job that unblemished timberlands play in supporting tiger populaces, we dive into the sensitive balance of these environments and the difficulties they face in a period of heightening human effect.

Regional Elements and Space for Meandering

One of the principal parts of Malayan tiger biology is the foundation and safeguard of domains inside flawless timberlands. Tigers are regional commonly, and the size of their domains is impacted by elements like prey overflow, water accessibility, and the thickness of different tigers. Perfect backwoods, with their immense fields of pristine scenes, give the essential space to tigers to lay out domains that meet their natural prerequisites.

In these undisturbed environments, tigers can wander openly, showing normal ways of behaving, for example, fragrance checking, vocalizations, and watching. The capacity to check and protect regions is critical for keeping a harmony between people, limiting contentions, and guaranteeing admittance to fundamental assets. Perfect woods consequently act as the material whereupon the unpredictable regional elements of Malayan tigers unfurl.

Prey Overflow and Biological system Wellbeing

Immaculate backwoods are described by elevated degrees of biodiversity, offering a rich embroidery of verdure. The overflow and variety of prey species inside these biological systems are fundamental for supporting Malayan tiger populaces. Deer, wild hog, and different ungulates flourish in the undisturbed climate, shaping the essential prey base for tigers.

The soundness of the prey populace straightforwardly relates with the strength of the tiger populace. Unblemished woods, with their flawless food networks and normal hunter prey connections, support a unique harmony among herbivores and carnivores. This environmental concordance guarantees that Malayan tigers approach an adequate and different exhibit of prey, meeting their dietary necessities and supporting the general wellbeing of the populace.

Protection of Hereditary Variety

Flawless woods assume a pivotal part in saving the hereditary variety of Malayan tiger populaces. Hereditary variety is essential for the drawn out practicality and flexibility of an animal types. In undisturbed natural surroundings, tigers have the space and opportunity to associate, working with hereditary trade between people. This trade is especially fundamental for forestalling the adverse consequences of inbreeding, like hereditary peculiarities and diminished conceptive wellness.

As tigers meander through unblemished timberlands, they add to the support of solid genetic stocks, guaranteeing that the populace holds the fundamental fluctuation to adjust to changing ecological circumstances. The protection of hereditary variety in these undisturbed scenes is a critical calculate the flexibility of Malayan tiger populaces against arising dangers, be they natural or anthropogenic.

Difficulties to Unblemished Woodlands: Deforestation and Fracture

Notwithstanding their urgent job, flawless woodlands face extreme dangers, principally determined by human exercises. Deforestation, driven by logging, horticultural extension, and foundation improvement, represents an immediate test to the trustworthiness of these undisturbed biological systems. As immaculate backwoods give way to human-overwhelmed scenes, the very establishment that supports Malayan tiger populaces is disintegrated.

Territory discontinuity intensifies the difficulties looked by flawless woods. Discontinuity happens when huge, persistent natural surroundings are partitioned into more modest, secluded patches. This interaction disturbs the normal network of biological systems, affecting the capacity of tigers to wander openly, lay out domains, and keep up with hereditary variety. Perfect woods, when broad and adjacent, become confined islands, powerless against the flowing impacts of natural surroundings misfortune.

Protection Techniques for Immaculate Timberlands

Saving the job of perfect backwoods in supporting Malayan tiger populaces requires exhaustive protection systems. Safeguarded regions and untamed life holds assume a basic part in protecting these undisturbed natural surroundings. Laying out and growing safeguarded regions guarantee that center tiger natural surroundings stay in one piece, giving the important space to regional elements, prey overflow, and hereditary trade.

Notwithstanding safeguarded regions, the making of untamed life hallways is fundamental for keeping up with network between confined patches of flawless woods. These hallways act as helps, permitting tigers to move between divided territories, moderating the adverse consequences of natural surroundings fracture. Cooperative endeavors between protection associations, states, and neighborhood networks are essential for the fruitful execution and support of these halls.

Practical Woodland The executives and Local area Commitment

Advancing maintainable timberland the executives rehearses is crucial for adjusting the requirements of human improvement with the basic to safeguard immaculate backwoods. Taking on feasible logging works on, implementing hostile to deforestation regulations, and boosting local area based preservation drives are viable techniques for alleviating the effect of human exercises on these basic environments.

Local area commitment is a foundation of effective preservation endeavors. Including neighborhood networks in the administration and security of perfect woodlands encourages a feeling of pride and obligation. Schooling programs that feature the significance of immaculate backwoods, for tigers as well as for the more extensive biological system and the prosperity of neighborhood networks, can make a common obligation to their safeguarding.

Mechanical Developments in Perfect Woods Protection

Progressions in innovation offer significant apparatuses for observing and rationing unblemished backwoods. Geographic Data Framework (GIS) and remote detecting advancements give definite guides of timberland cover, land use changes, and living space availability. Camera traps furnished with movement sensors offer experiences into the presence and conduct of Malayan tigers and their prey.

These mechanical developments empower traditionalists to settle on informed choices, focus on preservation endeavors, and track changes in unblemished timberland environments. The information gathered through these devices add to confirm based preservation techniques, guaranteeing that restricted assets are apportioned productively to address the most squeezing difficulties confronting these basic natural surroundings.

Worldwide Cooperation: A Worldwide Work to Save Immaculate Backwoods

Given the transboundary idea of Malayan tiger living spaces, global cooperation is central for the preservation of immaculate woods. Nations sharing tiger populaces should facilitate endeavors, share data, and altogether address the more extensive difficulties of living space misfortune and corruption. Worldwide associations, for example, the World Untamed life Asset (WWF) and the Worldwide Tiger Gathering, work with coordinated effort and channel assets toward extensive preservation drives.

The protection of perfect woodlands goes past public boundaries. It requires a worldwide obligation to reasonable turn of events, mindful utilization, and the acknowledgment of the natural worth of these environments. The global local area's help and coordinated effort are fundamental for guaranteeing that flawless woods keep on filling in as the life saver for Malayan tiger populaces and endless different species.

1.3 Overview of Malayan tiger behavior and reproduction

The Malayan tiger (Panthera tigris jacksoni) remains as a magnetic and confounding animal groups, encapsulating the substance of the thick, tropical scenes it calls home. Understanding the way of behaving and regenerative examples of this slippery large feline is significant for preservation endeavors pointed toward guaranteeing its drawn out endurance. In this investigation, we dive into the unpredictable features of Malayan tiger conduct, from singular territoriality to maternal sustaining, and the entrancing excursion of proliferation that shapes the eventual fate of this imperiled subspecies.

Lone Nature and Regional Way of behaving

One of the main qualities of Malayan tigers is their singular nature. Not at all like some other enormous feline species, Malayan tigers are known to carry on with overwhelmingly lone lives, with grown-up people laying out and savagely shielding their regions. The size of these regions fluctuates in light of elements like prey overflow, water accessibility, and the thickness of different tigers nearby.

Regional way of behaving is basic for keeping a harmony among people and limiting contentions over assets. Tigers utilize a blend of fragrance checking, vocalizations, and visual signs to lay out and convey regional limits. Aroma checking includes the testimony of pee or discharges from fragrance organs on trees, rocks, or other unmistakable elements inside their region. Vocalizations, including thunders and chuffing sounds, act as significant distance correspondence, permitting tigers to flag their presence to expected contenders.

This singular and regional way of life isn't only a conduct characteristic however a versatile system. It permits tigers to proficiently chase and secure prey inside their assigned domains, diminishing rivalry and staying away from clashes that could bring about wounds or fatalities.

Hunting and Taking care of Conduct

The Malayan tiger is a dominant hunter, situated at the head of the pecking order in its biological system. Hunting is a complicated and vital way of behaving, formed by the accessibility of prey and the tiger's information on its domain. Malayan tigers are crafty carnivores, with an eating regimen essentially comprising of ungulates like deer and wild hog. They are likewise known to go after more modest warm blooded animals and incidentally fish.

The hunting system includes a blend of following, ambushing, and an eruption of hazardous speed during the last pursuit. Tigers depend on their sharp feelings of sight and hearing to find prey, and their unmistakable coat designs give fantastic disguise in the thick vegetation of their environments.

When a kill is made, a Malayan tiger might drag its prey to a disconnected area inside its region. This conduct safeguards the kill from foragers as well as limits the possibilities experiencing different tigers during taking care of. Tigers are known to be strong swimmers, and in specific territories, they might try and chase in water, showing surprising flexibility in their hunting strategies.

Regenerative Way of behaving and Romance Customs

The regenerative way of behaving of Malayan tigers is an intriguing and critical part of their environment. Female tigers come into estrus, or intensity, for a short period, regularly going on around 3-6 days. During this time, they display explicit ways of behaving to flag their status to mate. These ways of behaving incorporate expanded vocalizations, fretfulness, and an uplifted interest in likely mates.

Male tigers, with their intense feeling of smell and attention to female estrus cycles, effectively watch their domains looking for open females. The romance ceremonies that unfurl when a male experiences a female in estrus are dazzling presentations of cat conduct. Romance might include common preparing, snuggling, and vocal cooperations. The pair participates in a dance of coordination and correspondence, laying out an association that goes before the mating act.

Mating can happen on different occasions during the female's estrus time frame, improving the probability of fruitful treatment. The copulatory way of behaving is a basic move toward the conceptive cycle, guaranteeing the exchange of sperm and the inception of the development time frame.

Growth and Birth

After a fruitful mating, the female enters an incubation period that endures roughly 93-112 days. The incubation time frame can fluctuate in light of variables like natural circumstances and the strength of the female. As the finish of the growth time frame draws near, the pregnant female starts to look for a reasonable cave site to conceive an offspring.

The introduction of Malayan tiger whelps is a pivotal occasion in the existence of a tigress. The offspring are generally conceived visually impaired and powerless, totally reliant upon their mom for sustenance and insurance. The litter size commonly goes from 2 to 4 fledglings, albeit bigger litters are not inconceivable.

The lair gives a solid and isolated space for the mother and her offspring. During the initial not many long stretches of their lives, the fledglings stay inside the lair, depending on their mom's milk for food.

The maternal senses of Malayan tigresses are exceptional, and they put huge investment in supporting and showing their whelps fundamental abilities to survive.

Maternal Consideration and Offspring Improvement

The time of maternal consideration is pivotal for the endurance and improvement of Malayan tiger whelps. The mother grooms and cleans her whelps, guaranteeing their cleanliness and prosperity. As the whelps develop, the mother acquaints them with strong food, carrying prey to the cave for the fledglings to work on hunting abilities.

The connection between a tigress and her fledglings is solid, and she wildly shields them from expected dangers. The whelps learn fundamental ways of behaving like hunting strategies, regional stamping, and the subtleties of correspondence from their mom. This time of maternal consideration go on for a long time until the fledglings are weaned and become more free.

Around the age of year and a half, Malayan tiger fledglings begin branching out all alone, progressively becoming independent trackers. This change denotes the start of their single lives, as they lay out domains and set out on their excursion to adulthood.

Difficulties to Regenerative Achievement: Human-Untamed life Struggle and Poaching

The conceptive outcome of Malayan tigers faces critical difficulties, generally coming from human exercises. Environment misfortune and fracture disturb the regular ways of behaving related with territoriality and mating. Tigers are constrained into nearer vicinity to human settlements, prompting an expansion in human-natural life clashes.

Human-untamed life clashes present dangers to both grown-up tigers and their offspring. Retaliatory killings because of predation on animals or saw dangers to human wellbeing are disturbing results of these struggles. Moreover, the discontinuity of environments lessens the accessible space for tigers to lay out domains, possibly prompting expanded contest for assets and a higher gamble of inbreeding.

Poaching addresses one more grave test to the conceptive outcome of Malayan tigers. The interest for tiger parts in customary medication and the unlawful untamed life exchange drive the focusing of these sublime animals. The deficiency of conceptive age people to poaching disturbs the sensitive equilibrium of tiger populaces and hampers the hereditary variety fundamental for their drawn out endurance.

Protection Techniques for Conduct and Propagation

The protection of Malayan tiger conduct and propagation requires an all encompassing and incorporated approach. Securing and reestablishing living spaces, laying out and keeping up with untamed life hallways, and tending to human-natural life clashes are principal for guaranteeing the normal ways of behaving related with territoriality and mating.

Hostile to poaching endeavors, severe policing, local area commitment are basic parts of systems pointed toward protecting Malayan tiger populaces. Schooling and mindfulness projects can assume a critical part in diminishing human-natural life clashes by encouraging comprehension and appreciation for the significance of these dominant hunters in keeping up with solid environments.

Reasonable improvement rehearses that focus on conjunction among people and tigers, alongside the advancement of capable the travel industry, add to establishing a helpful climate for the regular ways of behaving and conceptive outcome of Malayan tigers.

Mechanical Developments in Conduct and Generation Checking

Headways in innovation offer significant devices for checking the way of behaving and multiplication of Malayan tigers. Camera traps outfitted with movement sensors furnish analysts with bits of knowledge into the developments, ways of behaving, and populace elements of tigers in their normal territories. DNA examination takes into consideration the painless checking of hereditary variety and relatedness inside populaces.

Geographic Data Framework (GIS) and remote detecting advancements help in planning and observing tiger domains and territories. These apparatuses upgrade the comprehension of what living space changes and discontinuity mean for the regular ways of behaving of tigers and their capacity to replicate effectively.

CHAPTER 2

Habitat Fragmentation: Causes And Consequences

Living space discontinuity, an outcome of human exercises changing normal scenes, has arisen as one of the main dangers to worldwide biodiversity. The multifaceted and interconnected biological systems that once prospered are progressively being taken apart and changed into secluded patches. This interaction, driven by urbanization, horticulture, and foundation advancement, has significant results on the sensitive equilibrium of environments. In this investigation, we dig into the reasons for living space discontinuity and unwind the extensive ramifications for both vegetation.

Reasons for Environment Fracture

Urbanization and Framework Improvement:

Never-ending suburbia and the development of foundation are essential supporters of territory discontinuity. As urban communities extend and new streets, interstates, and improvements are developed, regular environments are taken apart into more modest, segregated pieces. The infringement of metropolitan regions into regular scenes upsets the coherence of biological systems and parts territories into pockets encompassed by human foundation.

Agrarian Extension:

The transformation of normal scenes into horticultural fields, manors, and pasturelands is a critical driver of environment discontinuity. Huge plots of timberlands are cleared for agribusiness, bringing about the production of divided patches of natural surroundings. The excess regular regions are frequently separated from one another, influencing the development of species and changing biological cycles.

Logging and Deforestation:

Logging exercises and broad deforestation add to the fracture of territories. The expulsion of enormous spans of woodlands for lumber or different assets abandons divided remainders. These detached patches are frequently lacking to help the first biodiversity, prompting a decrease in animal varieties lavishness and environment usefulness.

Mining Exercises:

Extractive ventures, including mining, modify scenes and add to natural surroundings fracture. The exhuming of minerals and assets can prompt the formation of open pits and adjusted geography, disturbing the normal network between territories. Moreover, the framework related with mining, like streets and offices, further parts environments.

Environmental Change:

While not an immediate reason for territory discontinuity, environmental change compounds its belongings. Adjustments in temperature and precipitation examples can drive species to move their reaches looking for appropriate environments. In divided scenes, these movements become testing, restricting the capacity of species to adjust and expanding the gamble of neighborhood annihilations.

Fire and Intrusive Species:

Regular unsettling influences, for example, rapidly spreading fires and the presentation of obtrusive species can add to territory discontinuity. Fires, whether normal or human-actuated, can make openings in biological systems, prompting fracture. Obtrusive species can outcompete local greenery, adjusting the design of environments and further dividing living spaces.

Results of Living space Discontinuity

Loss of Biodiversity:

One of the most prompt and extreme results of natural surroundings discontinuity is the deficiency of biodiversity. As natural surroundings are separated into more modest pieces, the populaces of different species become detached. This seclusion can prompt decreased hereditary variety inside populaces, making them more helpless against natural changes and less versatile to illnesses.

Disturbance of Biological Cycles:

Territory discontinuity upsets regular biological cycles that rely upon the availability of scenes. For instance, the development of species between natural surroundings is obstructed, influencing fertilization, seed dispersal, and hunter prey associations. These interruptions can have flowing impacts on the whole biological system, adjusting its construction and capability.

Edge Impacts:

The edges of divided natural surroundings, where one territory meets another or where an environment meets human framework, are vulnerable to edge impacts.

These impacts incorporate expanded openness to obtrusive species, modified microclimates, and more significant levels of human aggravation. Edge impacts can make conditions that are less positive for local species, further adding to biodiversity decline.

Expanded Human-Natural life Clashes:

Environment fracture frequently carries untamed life into closer vicinity to human settlements, prompting expanded human-natural life clashes. Species might wander into human-ruled regions looking for assets, bringing about clashes over food, space, and security. This can prompt negative impression of untamed life, frequently bringing about retaliatory killings or populace declines.

Decreased Living space Quality:

The more modest, confined sections coming about because of natural surroundings discontinuity by and large have diminished living space quality contrasted with flawless environments. These pieces may not give adequate assets like food, water, and appropriate rearing locales, prompting compromised conditions for the occupant species. This decrease in living space quality can upset the capacity of species to flourish and recreate.

Hereditary Confinement and Inbreeding:

With the discontinuity of living spaces, populaces of species become confined from one another. This separation can prompt hereditary float and diminished quality stream between populaces. After some time, this can bring about hereditary seclusion, expanding the gamble of inbreeding. Inbreeding can prompt diminished wellness, higher defenselessness to illnesses, and an improved probability of hereditary irregularities.

Disintegration of Environment Strength:

Divided scenes are frequently less versatile to ecological changes and aggravations. The capacity of environments to recuperate from normal occasions, like tempests or fierce blazes, is compromised when natural surroundings are divided. This disintegration of versatility makes biological systems more powerless against additional corruption and lessens their ability to adjust to evolving conditions.

Changed Species Elements:

The elements of species communications, including contest and predation, are changed in divided scenes. A few animal types might turn out to be more predominant, while others might decline or vanish completely. These progressions can upset the equilibrium that once existed in normal biological systems, prompting unusual and frequently unfortunate results.

Preservation Systems for Relieving Natural surroundings Discontinuity

Safeguarded Regions and Natural life Passageways:

Laying out and keeping up with safeguarded regions assume a critical part in preserving living spaces completely. Natural life passages, interfacing detached sections, work with the development of species between environments. These hallways are fundamental for keeping up with hereditary variety, empowering species to adjust to changing natural circumstances, and decreasing the adverse consequences of environment discontinuity.

Economical Land Use Arranging:

Carrying out economical land use arranging rehearses is fundamental for limiting the effect of natural surroundings discontinuity. Adjusting the requirements of human advancement with preservation needs includes recognizing regions reasonable for agribusiness, metropolitan turn of events, and framework projects while focusing on the security of basic living spaces.

Rebuilding and Reforestation:

Endeavors to reestablish and reforest corrupted scenes can help reconnect divided territories. Reforestation activities can reestablish biological network and upgrade the general nature of environments. Reclamation drives ought to zero in on establishing trees as well as on reestablishing the perplexing design and biodiversity of normal biological systems.

Green Foundation:

Integrating green foundation into metropolitan arranging can assist with relieving the impacts of living space fracture. Green rooftops, green walls, and metropolitan green spaces add to establishing natural surroundings availability inside metropolitan conditions. This coordinated methodology upholds both human prosperity and biodiversity protection.

Local area Commitment and Instruction:

Connecting with nearby networks in preservation endeavors is vital for the progress of living space assurance drives. Teaching people group about the significance of biodiversity, the results of living space discontinuity, and maintainable practices cultivates a feeling of stewardship. Networks that get it and value their job in protection are bound to help and partake in endeavors to moderate natural surroundings fracture.

Untamed life Amicable Advancement Practices:

Taking on natural life amicable advancement rehearses includes planning framework projects with thought for untamed life development and living space network.

For instance, integrating natural life intersections over streets and roadways can assist with decreasing the effect of straight boundaries on species development.

Worldwide Cooperation and Strategy Support:

Territory discontinuity is a worldwide issue that requires global coordinated effort. Supporting for strategies that focus on territory protection, manageable turn of events, and the relief of environmental change on a worldwide scale is fundamental. Protection associations, states, and worldwide bodies assume a basic part in molding and executing strategies that address the main drivers of living space discontinuity.

Mechanical Advancements for Observing:

Trend setting innovations, like satellite symbolism, remote detecting, and Geographic Data Framework (GIS) instruments, give significant information to observing natural surroundings discontinuity. These apparatuses empower researchers and protectionists to survey scene changes, distinguish divided regions, and focus on preservation endeavors in light of information driven bits of knowledge.

2.1 Definition and explanation

Territory discontinuity is a term that embodies the significant modifications happening in regular scenes because of human exercises, bringing about the division of once persistent living spaces into more modest, separated patches. This peculiarity has turned into a crucial idea in environment and protection science, mirroring the many-sided exchange between human turn of events and the fragile equilibrium of biological systems. In this complete investigation, we dive into the meaning of natural surroundings discontinuity and proposition a nuanced clarification of its causes, outcomes, and the continuous endeavors to relieve its effect on worldwide biodiversity.

Meaning of Natural surroundings Fracture:

Natural surroundings fracture alludes to the interaction by which huge, adjoining territories are partitioned into more modest, secluded sections, frequently isolated by human-changed scenes. These sections might appear as patches, leftovers, or islands, encompassed by areas of adjusted or created land. The critical trait of living space fracture is the disturbance of normal coherence, prompting spatial irregularity in biological systems that were once interconnected.

This fracture can happen across different kinds of living spaces, including woods, fields, wetlands, and marine conditions. A consequence of human exercises change scenes for purposes like urbanization, horticulture, framework improvement, logging, and mining. The results of territory discontinuity stretch out past the actual change of scenes, influencing the natural cycles, species associations, and biodiversity inside impacted regions.

Reasons for Living space Fracture:

Urbanization and Framework Improvement:

Never-ending suburbia and the development of framework, including streets, parkways, and neighborhoods, are conspicuous reasons for natural surroundings fracture. As urban areas and human settlements grow, regular territories are analyzed and changed into more modest, disconnected parts encompassed by urbanized scenes.

Agrarian Extension:

The transformation of regular scenes into rural fields and estates is a huge driver of territory discontinuity. Enormous scope getting free from backwoods for agribusiness brings about the production of divided natural surroundings, upsetting the first congruity of biological systems.

Logging and Deforestation:

Logging exercises, driven by the interest for lumber and other timberland items, add to the fracture of regular territories. The evacuation of huge parts of woodlands prompts the production of confined patches, influencing the biodiversity and biological cycles related with flawless environments.

Mining Exercises:

Extractive enterprises, like mining, change scenes and add to living space fracture. Open-pit mining, deforestation related with mining exercises, and the production of foundation for mining activities all add to the interruption of normal territories.

Environmental Change:

While not an immediate reason, environmental change can intensify living space fracture. Changes in temperature, precipitation examples, and ocean levels might drive species to move their reaches, affecting the availability of environments. Environment prompted territory movements can bring about divided scenes that obstruct species transformation.

Fire and Obtrusive Species:

Regular aggravations, like rapidly spreading fires, can make openings in environments, prompting discontinuity. The presentation of obtrusive species can additionally compound the impacts by adjusting the piece and construction of normal living spaces.

Outcomes of Environment Fracture:

Loss of Biodiversity:

One of the main outcomes of environment fracture is the deficiency of biodiversity. The detachment of populaces inside divided patches can prompt diminished hereditary variety, making species more powerless against natural changes and less strong to illnesses.

Disturbance of Biological Cycles:

Living space discontinuity upsets regular environmental cycles that depend on the network of scenes. The development of species between natural surroundings, fundamental for processes like fertilization and seed dispersal, is obstructed. This disturbance has flowing consequences for biological system elements.

Edge Impacts:

The edges of divided territories, where one territory meets another or where an environment meets human framework, are powerless to edge impacts. These impacts incorporate modified microclimates, expanded openness to intrusive species, and more significant levels of human unsettling influence, making conditions less great for local species.

Expanded Human-Untamed life Clashes:

Territory discontinuity frequently carries natural life into closer vicinity to human settlements, prompting expanded human-natural life clashes. Species might wander into human-ruled regions looking for assets, bringing about clashes over food, space, and security.

Decreased Environment Quality:

Divided living spaces for the most part have diminished quality contrasted with flawless environments. The more modest, disengaged sections may not give adequate assets like food, water, and reasonable reproducing locales, prompting compromised conditions for inhabitant species.

Hereditary Disengagement and Inbreeding:

The disengagement of populaces inside divided living spaces can prompt hereditary separation. Diminished quality stream between populaces builds the gamble of inbreeding, which can bring about decreased wellness, higher defenselessness to illnesses, and an improved probability of hereditary irregularities.

Disintegration of Environment Flexibility:

Divided scenes are frequently less versatile to ecological changes and unsettling influences. The capacity of biological systems to recuperate from normal occasions, like tempests or fierce blazes, is compromised when living spaces are divided, making environments more powerless against additional corruption.

Adjusted Species Elements:

Fracture modifies the elements of species collaborations, including contest and predation. A few animal groups might turn out to be more prevailing, while others might decline or vanish completely. These progressions can disturb the equilibrium that once existed in regular biological systems, prompting erratic and frequently unfortunate results.

Alleviation and Preservation Endeavors:

Safeguarded Regions and Natural life Hallways:

Laying out and keeping up with safeguarded regions are principal for saving living spaces completely. Natural life passages, which associate disconnected sections, work with the development of species between territories, keeping up with hereditary variety and lessening the adverse consequences of fracture.

Maintainable Land Use Arranging:

Executing reasonable land use arranging rehearses includes recognizing regions appropriate for human turn of events and preservation. Adjusting the necessities of human populaces with protection needs is fundamental for limiting the effect of environment discontinuity.

Rebuilding and Reforestation:

Endeavors to reestablish and reforest corrupted scenes can help reconnect divided territories. Reclamation projects mean to reestablish environmental network and improve the general nature of living spaces, adding to the protection of biodiversity.

Green Framework:

Integrating green framework into metropolitan arranging mitigates the impacts of territory fracture inside metropolitan conditions. Green rooftops, green walls, and metropolitan green spaces add to making territory availability and supporting biodiversity protection.

Local area Commitment and Instruction:

Connecting with neighborhood networks in preservation endeavors is vital for the outcome of territory security drives. Teaching people group about the significance of biodiversity, the outcomes of living space fracture, and supportable practices encourages a feeling of stewardship.

Untamed life Cordial Advancement Practices:

Natural life amicable advancement rehearses include planning foundation projects with thought for natural life development and living space network. Measures, for example, untamed life intersections over streets can assist with lessening the effect of direct boundaries on species development.

Worldwide Cooperation and Strategy Support:

Pushing for strategies that focus on territory preservation, manageable turn of events, and environmental change moderation on a worldwide scale is pivotal. Global joint effort and the inclusion of states and protection associations are fundamental for tending to the main drivers of living space fracture.

Mechanical Developments for Checking:

Cutting edge innovations, including satellite symbolism, remote detecting, and Geographic Data Framework (GIS) apparatuses, give important information to observing living space fracture. These apparatuses empower researchers and traditionalists to survey scene changes, distinguish divided regions, and focus on preservation endeavors in view of information driven experiences.

2.2 Human activities leading to habitat fragmentation

Environment fracture, a result of human exercises reshaping normal scenes, has arisen as a basic natural test. The complex snare of life that once prospered in adjoining living spaces is progressively disentangling, as huge territories of regular environments are changed into disengaged patches. This discontinuity, driven by different human exercises, has expansive results on biodiversity, biological system elements, and the fragile equilibrium of our planet. In this investigation, we dive into the significant human exercises prompting environment discontinuity, revealing insight into the cycles that reshape the regular world.

1. Urbanization and Foundation Advancement:

   Urbanization, the development of urban areas and human settlements, remains as an unmistakable driver of natural surroundings fracture. As populaces develop, so does the interest for lodging, streets, and other foundation. Immense areas of regular living spaces are cleared to clear a path for metropolitan turn of events, bringing about the division of once nonstop scenes into more modest, detached pieces.

   Streets and thruways, fundamental for availability in urbanized regions, further fuel living space discontinuity. They go about as direct hindrances, cutting through territories and making secluded pockets of environments. The related foundation, like structures, spans, and other human-made structures, intensifies the fracture, leaving an interwoven of territories encompassed by never-ending suburbia.

2. Agrarian Extension:

   The transformation of regular scenes into horticultural regions is a critical supporter of living space discontinuity. Enormous scope getting free from timberlands and different environments to clear a path for croplands, ranches, and pastures prompts the making of detached sections. The excess regular environments are frequently restricted to patches encircled by immense spans of rural land. Monoculture rehearses, where huge regions are committed to a solitary yield, further heighten the effect of farming extension. This homogenization of scenes decreases the variety of territories and disturbs the environmental cycles that rely upon differed and interconnected biological systems.

3. **Logging and Deforestation:**

Logging exercises, driven by the interest for lumber and other woodland items, assume a crucial part in environment fracture. The evacuation of huge areas of woods not just lessens the general degree of normal environments yet in addition brings about the formation of divided patches. These confined remainders are frequently deficient to help the different greenery that once flourished in flawless environments.

Deforestation, driven by variables like horticulture, logging, and framework improvement, intensifies the effects of environment discontinuity. The deficiency of essential woodlands, with their many-sided trap of life, abandons divided scenes helpless against a bunch of natural outcomes.

4. **Mining Exercises:**

Extractive ventures, including mining, modify scenes and contribute essentially to territory discontinuity. Open-pit mining, specifically, brings about huge unearthings that make actual hindrances inside environments. The framework related with mining, like streets, offices, and extraction destinations, further parts territories and upsets normal availability.

Mining exercises adjust the actual construction of scenes as well as present toxins and unsettling influences that can lastingly affect environments. The mix of territory annihilation and contamination heightens the difficulties looked by species living in and around mining regions.

5. **Agribusiness Prompted Discontinuity in Oceanic Biological systems:**

Territory fracture isn't restricted to earthbound conditions; amphibian biological systems additionally experience disturbances because of human exercises. Farming, through practices like dam development and channelization of waterways, can section oceanic living spaces. Dams, specifically, make actual hindrances in streams, adjusting the regular stream and availability of sea-going biological systems.

Channelization, pointed toward forestalling flooding and upgrading farming efficiency, fixes and limits streams, disturbing the different environments that normally structure along wandering conduits. These adjustments can influence fish relocation, modify dregs transport, and lead to the deficiency of wetland territories.

6. Framework Extension in Seaside Regions:
   Waterfront regions are not resistant to the effects of natural surroundings fracture coming about because of human exercises. Framework advancement in seaside zones, including ports, resorts, and neighborhoods, frequently prompts the adjustment and fracture of normal living spaces like mangroves, salt swamps, and coral reefs. Waterfront improvement can disturb the availability of biological systems basic for marine life. Coral reefs, for instance, give fundamental territories to a heap of animal types, and their discontinuity because of seaside improvement undermines the biodiversity and biological capabilities they support.

7. Environmental Change-Actuated Reach Movements:
   While not an immediate reason for environment discontinuity, environmental change impacts the circulation of species and can intensify fracture impacts. Changes in temperature, precipitation examples, and ocean levels force species to move their reaches looking for reasonable territories. In divided scenes, these movements become testing, restricting the capacity of species to adjust and expanding the gamble of neighborhood eradications.

   Environment prompted territory movements can bring about the production of segregated patches of appropriate living space encompassed by cold or unacceptable circumstances. This further convolutes the preservation and the executives of species previously wrestling with the outcomes of natural surroundings fracture.

8. Fire and Intrusive Species:

Normal aggravations, like rapidly spreading fires, can add to natural surroundings discontinuity, especially when they bring about the formation of open patches inside environments. While fierce blazes are a characteristic piece of numerous environments, human exercises, for example, fire concealment and land-use changes can modify the recurrence and power of flames, prompting fracture.

The presentation of obtrusive species, frequently worked with by human exercises, can intensify the effects of natural surroundings discontinuity. Obtrusive species may outcompete local verdure, modifying the construction and sythesis of environments and further adding to the debasement of regular natural surroundings.

Outcomes of Human-Initiated Living space Discontinuity:

Loss of Biodiversity:

Maybe the main outcome of living space discontinuity is the deficiency of biodiversity. The confinement of populaces inside divided patches can prompt diminished hereditary variety, making species more powerless against natural changes and less versatile to sicknesses.

Interruption of Natural Cycles:

Natural surroundings fracture disturbs fundamental environmental cycles that rely upon the network of scenes. The development of species between natural surroundings is obstructed, affecting cycles like fertilization, seed dispersal, and hunter prey cooperations.

Edge Impacts:

The edges of divided natural surroundings, where one living space meets another or where an environment meets human foundation, are defenseless to edge impacts. These incorporate modified microclimates, expanded openness to obtrusive species, and more significant levels of human aggravation, making conditions less positive for local species.

Expanded Human-Natural life Clashes:

Living space fracture frequently carries untamed life into closer nearness to human settlements, prompting expanded human-natural life clashes. Species might wander into human-ruled regions looking for assets, bringing about clashes over food, space, and wellbeing.

Decreased Natural surroundings Quality:

Divided environments by and large have decreased quality contrasted with unblemished biological systems. The more modest, segregated parts may not give adequate assets like food, water, and appropriate rearing destinations, prompting compromised conditions for inhabitant species.

Hereditary Seclusion and Inbreeding:

The seclusion of populaces inside divided natural surroundings can prompt hereditary confinement. Diminished quality stream between populaces expands the gamble of inbreeding, which can bring about decreased wellness, higher defenselessness to sicknesses, and an improved probability of hereditary irregularities.

Disintegration of Environment Versatility:

Divided scenes are frequently less versatile to ecological changes and unsettling influences. The capacity of biological systems to recuperate from normal occasions, like tempests or out of control fires, is compromised when living spaces are divided, making environments more powerless against additional corruption.

Adjusted Species Elements:

Natural surroundings discontinuity adjusts the elements of species associations, including contest and predation. A few animal varieties might turn out to be more prevailing, while others might decline or vanish completely. These progressions can upset the equilibrium that once existed in regular biological systems, prompting erratic and frequently bothersome outcomes.

Relief and Preservation Techniques:

Safeguarded Regions and Untamed life Hallways:

Laying out and keeping up with safeguarded regions assume a pivotal part in moderating living space fracture. Untamed life hallways, interfacing segregated parts, work with the development of species between living spaces, keeping up with hereditary variety and diminishing the adverse consequences of fracture.

Practical Land Use Arranging:

Executing maintainable land use arranging rehearses is fundamental for limiting the effect of living space fracture. Adjusting the requirements of human advancement with preservation needs includes recognizing regions reasonable for farming, metropolitan turn of events, and framework projects while focusing on the security of basic territories.

Reclamation and Reforestation:

Endeavors to reestablish and reforest debased scenes can help reconnect divided living spaces. Rebuilding projects plan to reestablish biological availability and upgrade the general nature of environments, adding to the preservation of biodiversity.

Green Foundation:

Integrating green foundation into metropolitan arranging mitigates the impacts of living space discontinuity inside metropolitan conditions. Green rooftops, green walls, and metropolitan green spaces add to making natural surroundings network and supporting biodiversity protection.

Local area Commitment and Instruction:

Connecting with nearby networks in preservation endeavors is urgent for the progress of territory security drives. Instructing people group about the significance of biodiversity, the outcomes of natural surroundings fracture, and feasible practices encourages a feeling of stewardship.

Untamed life Well disposed Improvement Practices:

Taking on natural life agreeable improvement rehearses includes planning foundation projects with thought for natural life development and environment availability. Measures, for example, untamed life intersections over streets can assist with diminishing the effect of direct boundaries on species development.

Worldwide Cooperation and Strategy Support:

Pushing for strategies that focus on living space preservation, feasible turn of events, and environmental change relief on a worldwide scale is critical. Global cooperation and the contribution of states and protection associations are fundamental for tending to the main drivers of environment discontinuity.

Mechanical Advancements for Checking:

Trend setting innovations, including satellite symbolism, remote detecting, and Geographic Data Framework (GIS) devices, give important information to checking natural surroundings discontinuity. These instruments empower researchers and protectionists to survey scene changes, distinguish divided regions, and focus on preservation endeavors in view of information driven bits of knowledge.

CHAPTER 3

Impact Of Habitat Fragmentation On Malayan Tiger Populations

Environment fracture, an outcome of human exercises reshaping normal scenes, has arisen as a basic danger to the endurance of different species, including the glorious Malayan tiger (Panthera tigris jacksoni). As the thick tropical backwoods of the Malay Promontory change into divided patches encompassed by human-adjusted conditions, the complicated dance of life for Malayan tigers turns out to be progressively problematic. In this investigation, we dive into the particular effects of territory discontinuity on Malayan tiger populaces, disentangling the intricacies of this dangerous excursion and the dire requirement for preservation endeavors to get their future.

**1. Meaning of Malayan Tigers:

Prior to diving into the effects of environment fracture, understanding the interesting qualities of Malayan tigers is vital. Logically known as Panthera tigris jacksoni, these tigers are a subspecies of the Indo-Chinese tiger (Panthera tigris corbetti). Malayan tigers are basically tracked down in the southern piece of the Malay Promontory, occupying a scope of environments from marsh timberlands to rugged locales. With particular highlights like a dynamic orange coat, more obscure stripes, and a vigorous form, Malayan tigers are very much adjusted to their tropical natural surroundings.

**2. Normal Territory of Malayan Tigers:

The normal living space of Malayan tigers includes thick and different tropical backwoods, going from marsh rainforests to montane woods at higher heights. These territories furnish the tigers with more than adequate prey, including deer, wild pig, and different ungulates. The intricacy of these environments is indispensable to the natural equilibrium that supports Malayan tiger populaces.

****3. The Danger of Natural surroundings Fracture:**
Natural surroundings fracture unfurls as human exercises, like logging, farming, and foundation improvement, change enormous, persistent territories into more modest, segregated sections. For Malayan tigers, this discontinuity represents a diverse danger, disturbing their regular ways of behaving, restricting their admittance to assets, and expanding the gamble of human-untamed life clashes.

****4. Influence on Tiger Development and Home Reach:**
Malayan tigers are known for their broad home reaches, which are urgent for their endurance and propagation. Environment fracture upsets the regular development examples of tigers, limiting their capacity to navigate enormous regions. The divided scene frequently brings about more modest and more detached domains, prompting expanded contest among people for restricted assets.

Tigers, ordinarily, are singular and regional creatures. The accessibility of adequate room is fundamental for keeping up with sound populace elements and lessening between species clashes. At the point when environment fracture limits tigers to more modest regions, it can prompt expanded pressure, diminished regenerative achievement, and a higher probability of hereditary inbreeding inside segregated populaces.

****5. Hereditary Segregation and Inbreeding:**
One of the most significant effects of natural surroundings discontinuity on Malayan tiger populaces is the gamble of hereditary disconnection and inbreeding. As environments become detached sections, tiger populaces inside these patches are cut off from one another. This segregation restricts the normal quality stream between populaces, improving the probability of inbreeding.

Inbreeding presents critical dangers to the wellbeing and wellness of Malayan tigers. It can prompt diminished hereditary variety, making populaces more vulnerable to illnesses and less versatile to natural changes. Over the long haul, inbreeding can bring about the declaration of hurtful latent attributes, compromising the general suitability of the populace.

****6. Changed Prey Accessibility and Hunting Examples:**
Living space discontinuity influences tigers straightforwardly as well as upsets the overflow and circulation of their prey. The change of regular scenes into divided fixes frequently prompts changes in the circulation of ungulates and other prey species. This, thusly, changes the hunting examples of Malayan tigers, driving them to adjust to a scene where prey accessibility is lopsided.

In divided territories, tigers might confront difficulties in getting to customary hunting grounds, and the diminished accessibility of prey might prompt expanded rivalry among people. The modified elements of hunter prey communications can have flowing consequences for the whole environment, influencing the overflow and conduct of the two tigers and their prey.

**7. Human-Natural life Clashes:

As environment fracture carries Malayan tigers into closer vicinity to human settlements, the potential for human-natural life clashes escalates. Tigers might wander into human-ruled regions looking for food, particularly when regular prey is scant inside divided environments. This causes what is going on for the two tigers and nearby networks.

Human-natural life clashes can bring about retaliatory killings of tigers by networks trying to safeguard their animals and guarantee their security. Moreover, the presence of tigers close to human settlements represents an endanger to living souls, further heightening strains between protection objectives and the wellbeing worries of neighborhood populaces.

**8. Decreased Versatility to Ecological Changes:

Divided living spaces are frequently less versatile to ecological changes, including environment varieties and catastrophic events. The capacity of Malayan tigers to adjust to changing ecological circumstances is compromised when their environments are divided. More modest, disconnected populaces are more defenseless against stochastic occasions, for example, sickness episodes or outrageous climate occasions, which can have extreme ramifications for their endurance.

Preservation Methodologies for Malayan Tigers in Divided Environments:

Safeguarded Regions and Hallway Availability:

Laying out and extending safeguarded regions assume a urgent part in protecting the excess natural surroundings of Malayan tigers. These regions ought to be decisively associated through untamed life hallways, taking into consideration the development of people between disconnected sections. Hallway network is imperative for keeping up with hereditary variety, diminishing inbreeding, and working with the regular ways of behaving of tigers.

Reasonable Land Use Arranging:

Executing supportable land use arranging rehearses is fundamental for adjusting the necessities of human advancement with the protection of Malayan tiger environments. Distinguishing and safeguarding basic natural surroundings, especially those with high tiger densities, mitigates the effect of environment fracture.

Local area Commitment and Training:

Connecting with neighborhood networks in protection endeavors is essential for encouraging concurrence among people and Malayan tigers.

Training programs that feature the significance of tigers in keeping up with environmental equilibrium, combined with drives that address human-untamed life clashes, can add to the help of protection objectives.

Hostile to Poaching and Policing:

Fortifying enemy of poaching endeavors and upholding untamed life assurance regulations are fundamental parts of Malayan tiger preservation. Poaching for tiger parts and retaliatory killings because of contentions present direct dangers to tiger populaces. Hearty policing and local area association in natural life security add to the discouragement of criminal operations.

Exploration and Checking:

Persistent exploration and checking endeavors are pivotal for grasping the way of behaving, populace elements, and wellbeing of Malayan tigers in divided environments. Trend setting innovations, for example, camera traps, satellite following, and hereditary examination, give significant bits of knowledge to preservation arranging and the board.

Living space Reclamation and Reforestation:

Drives zeroed in on living space reclamation and reforestation expect to reconnect divided scenes and upgrade the general nature of tiger environments. Reforestation projects add to the making of adjoining environments, furnishing tigers with bigger domains and supporting the assorted cluster of species that comprise their regular prey.

Worldwide Cooperation and Support:

Malayan tiger preservation is a worldwide obligation that requires coordinated effort between legislatures, protection associations, and the global local area. Backing for strategies that focus on territory protection, economical turn of events, and environmental change alleviation is essential for tending to the underlying drivers of living space discontinuity.

3.1 Reduced available habitat

Diminished accessible territory is a basic result of human exercises that reshape the scenes we possess. As normal spaces recoil, environments go through significant changes, prompting sweeping ramifications for biodiversity, species communications, and the general wellbeing of the planet. In this investigation, we dig into the intricacies of diminished accessible territory, analyzing the causes behind this peculiarity, its effects on different environments, and the basic for protection endeavors to alleviate its extensive impacts.

1. Meaning of Decreased Accessible Environment:
Decreased accessible living space alludes to the lessened span of indigenous habitats that are appropriate for the endurance and food of different species. This decrease is principally determined by human exercises like urbanization, agribusiness, deforestation, and foundation advancement, which change once far reaching and interconnected environments into more modest, divided patches. The results of this decrease reach out past the quick actual changes to the scene, impacting the elements of environments and the mind boggling trap of life that depends on assorted and broad territories.

2. Reasons for Diminished Accessible Territory:
Urbanization and Framework Improvement:
The extension of metropolitan regions and the development of framework, including streets, interstates, and structures, lead to the change of regular scenes into created spaces. This change brings about the fracture and decrease of accessible environment for endless species, from bugs and plants to bigger vertebrates and birds.

Horticultural Extension:
The transformation of regular natural surroundings into rural land to fulfill the developing need for food is a significant supporter of decreased accessible environment. Enormous scope getting free from timberlands and different environments for cultivating decreases the space accessible for local vegetation, upsetting natural cycles and species communications.

Deforestation and Logging:
Deforestation, driven by logging and land freedom for different purposes, brings about the immediate deficiency of broad forested regions. The expulsion of trees and modification of timberland scenes decrease the accessible natural surroundings for a large number of animal categories, compromising biodiversity and the environment benefits that woods give.

Mining Exercises:
Extractive businesses, like mining, adjust scenes and add to decreased accessible living space. Open-pit mining, specifically, brings about the obliteration of huge regions, making actual boundaries inside biological systems and restricting the space for regular environments to persevere.

Environmental Change:
While not an immediate reason, environmental change can in a roundabout way add to diminished accessible living space. Changes in temperature, precipitation examples, and ocean levels can adjust

the dispersion of territories, driving species to move their reaches. These movements might bring about the decrease and fracture of appropriate territories.

Framework Extension in Beach front Regions:

Beach front turn of events, including the development of ports, resorts, and local locations, can prompt the change and discontinuity of seaside territories. Mangroves, salt bogs, and coral reefs, fundamental for marine biodiversity, may encounter decreased accessible territory because of human exercises in seaside zones.

Fire and Obtrusive Species:

Normal aggravations like fierce blazes, frequently exacerbated by human exercises, can make openings in biological systems, bringing about the decrease of accessible natural surroundings. The presentation of intrusive species further adds to territory debasement, adjusting the organization and construction of regular habitats.

3. Outcomes of Decreased Accessible Environment:

Loss of Biodiversity:

Maybe the main outcome of diminished accessible territory is the deficiency of biodiversity. The decrease in space appropriate for different species prompts decreases in populaces and, now and again, nearby eliminations. The unpredictable snare of connections between species is disturbed, influencing the equilibrium and strength of biological systems.

Disturbance of Environmental Cycles:

Decreased accessible natural surroundings upsets fundamental environmental cycles that rely upon the network and variety of scenes. The development of species between environments, fundamental for cycles like fertilization, seed dispersal, and hunter prey connections, is hindered. This interruption has flowing consequences for the working of biological systems.

Expanded Natural surroundings Discontinuity:

The decrease of accessible natural surroundings frequently brings about expanded living space fracture. As regular scenes are changed into more modest, detached patches, the availability between territories is upset. This discontinuity can prompt a scope of natural issues, including hereditary separation, modified species elements, and expanded weakness to ecological changes.

Adjusted Species Elements:

The elements of species associations are altogether changed notwithstanding decreased accessible living space. Rivalry for restricted assets heightens, prompting changes in the dissemination and

overflow of species. A few animal types might turn out to be
more predominant, while others might decline or vanish completely,
making irregular characteristics in biological systems.

Expanded Human-Natural life Clashes:

Decreased accessible living space frequently carries natural life into
closer nearness to human settlements, improving the probability
of human-untamed life clashes. As normal spaces shrivel, species
might wander into human-ruled regions looking for assets, prompting clashes an over area, food, and wellbeing.

Loss of Biological system Administrations:

Biological systems offer fundamental types of assistance, like clean
water, fertilization of harvests, and guideline of environment. Decreased accessible natural surroundings compromises the capacity
of biological systems to convey these administrations. The deficiency of assorted natural surroundings reduces the limit of biological systems to help human prosperity and keep up with ecological
equilibrium.

Hereditary Confinement and Inbreeding:

Decreased accessible environment can prompt the separation of
populaces, restricting quality stream between them. This hereditary
disengagement expands the gamble of inbreeding, which can bring
about diminished hereditary variety, lower wellness, and expanded
helplessness to illnesses.

Decreased Strength to Ecological Changes:

Biological systems with decreased accessible territory are frequently
less versatile to natural changes and unsettling influences. The
capacity of environments to recuperate from occasions like out of
control fires, tempests, or sickness episodes is compromised when
living spaces are divided and decreased in size.

4. Protection Systems for Relieving Diminished Accessible Territory:

Safeguarded Regions and Availability:

Laying out and growing safeguarded regions assume an essential part
in monitoring natural surroundings. These regions act as shelters for
different species and can assist with relieving the effects of decreased
accessible living space. Moreover, making untamed life hallways to associate detached sections works with the development of species, keeping
up with hereditary variety and environmental availability.

Feasible Land Use Arranging:

Carrying out reasonable land use arranging rehearses is fundamental
for limiting the effect of diminished accessible territory. Adjusting the

necessities of human improvement with preservation needs includes recognizing and safeguarding basic environments while advancing mindful land use rehearses.

Reclamation and Reforestation:

Endeavors to reestablish and reforest debased scenes can add to the development of accessible living space. Reclamation drives ought to zero in on establishing local vegetation, reestablishing biological system structure, and improving network between divided patches.

Green Foundation in Metropolitan Preparation:

Integrating green framework into metropolitan arranging mitigates the impacts of diminished accessible living space inside metropolitan conditions. Green rooftops, green walls, and metropolitan green spaces add to making natural surroundings availability and supporting biodiversity preservation in urban communities and human-ruled regions.

Local area Commitment and Schooling:

Drawing in neighborhood networks in preservation endeavors is vital for the outcome of living space assurance drives. Instructing people group about the significance of biodiversity, the results of diminished accessible natural surroundings, and feasible practices cultivates a feeling of stewardship.

Natural life Well disposed Improvement Practices:

Embracing untamed life well disposed advancement rehearses includes planning framework projects with thought for untamed life development and territory network. Consolidating highlights, for example, untamed life intersections over streets and thruways can assist with decreasing the effect of direct hindrances on species development.

Worldwide Cooperation and Strategy Promotion:

Supporting for strategies that focus on living space protection, practical turn of events, and environmental change relief on a worldwide scale is critical. Worldwide cooperation and the association of state run administrations, NGOs, and the confidential area are fundamental for tending to the underlying drivers of decreased accessible territory.

Mechanical Advancements for Checking:

Trend setting innovations, including satellite symbolism, remote detecting, and Geographic Data Framework (GIS) apparatuses, give important information to observing diminished accessible living space. These devices empower researchers and protectionists to survey scene changes, recognize divided regions, and focus on preservation endeavors in view of information driven bits of knowledge.

3.2 Isolation of tiger populations

The disconnection of tiger populaces is a grave result of living space discontinuity, a peculiarity driven by human exercises that change once-constant territories into divided patches. As these notable huge felines explore the disconnected scenes, the ramifications are significant, addressing the hereditary wellbeing, environmental elements, and generally endurance of these great species.

1. Hereditary Detachment and Inbreeding:
   Maybe the most prompt concern emerging from the confinement of tiger populaces is the gamble of hereditary detachment and inbreeding. Natural surroundings fracture makes actual boundaries that confine the development of tigers between separated patches. This separation limits quality stream between populaces, prompting diminished hereditary variety inside every populace. Inbreeding, an outcome of mating between firmly related people, can bring about the outflow of harmful qualities, debilitated insusceptible frameworks, and diminished generally wellness. The drawn out reasonability of detached tiger populaces turns out to be progressively problematic as hereditary variety decreases.

2. Confined Home Reaches and Regional Battles:
   Tigers are known for their sweeping home reaches, fundamental for getting adequate assets and guaranteeing regenerative achievement. The disengagement of populaces prompts the restriction of tigers inside more modest regions, escalating regional battles. As rivalry for restricted space and assets elevates, clashes between people become more successive, disturbing normal ways of behaving and focusing on the populaces. The subsequent regional imperatives additionally influence the capacity of tigers to take part in fundamental exercises like hunting, rearing, and laying out domains for their posterity.

3. Impeded Movement and Network:
   Availability between tiger environments is basic for keeping up with sound populaces and advancing hereditary trade. Territory discontinuity disturbs regular relocation courses and obstructs the development of tigers between separated patches.
   This impeded network not just restricts the capacity of people to track down mates yet additionally obstructs the normal dispersal of sub-grown-ups looking for new domains. As an outcome, disengaged populaces face the test of supporting hereditary variety, making them more helpless against natural changes and illnesses.

4. Changed Prey-Hunter Elements:
   The disconnection of tiger populaces has flowing consequences for

the elements of prey-hunter communications. In divided scenes, the two tigers and their prey might encounter adjusted conveyance designs. Prey species might find shelter in confined patches, prompting limited overgrazing or herbivore pressure. Tigers, thusly, may confront difficulties in getting to conventional hunting grounds, affecting their capacity to supply secure a satisfactory food. The subsequent irregularity in prey-hunter elements can have far reaching influences all through the environment, impacting vegetation, biodiversity, and the generally biological strength of the scene.

5. Expanded Weakness to Elimination:
The detachment of tiger populaces hoists their weakness to elimination. Little and detached populaces are more helpless to stochastic occasions, like infection episodes or catastrophic events. The absence of hereditary variety diminishes the versatile capability of these populaces, making them less strong to ecological changes. Also, the combined effects of environment discontinuity, including human-untamed life clashes and poaching, further compound the dangers looked by segregated tiger populaces.

6. Preservation Difficulties and Arrangements:

Tending to the detachment of tiger populaces requires deliberate protection endeavors that focus on scene network and natural surroundings conservation. The foundation and support of untamed life passages, decisively interfacing segregated patches, assume an essential part in working with the development of tigers. Safeguarded regions, planned with a comprehension of tiger home reaches, act as safe-havens for these lofty felines. Preservation drives should likewise think about the more extensive scene setting, upholding for practical land use arranging and moderating human-untamed life clashes.

3.3 Increased human-tiger conflicts

The heightening of human-tiger clashes remains as a distinct outcome of natural surroundings fracture, infringement into untamed life territories, and the resulting decrease of accessible space for the two people and tigers. As these superb hunters explore progressively divided scenes, experiences with human settlements become more incessant, prompting an unsafe dance of endurance for the two species.

The essential driver of increased human-tiger clashes is the infringement of human settlements into customary tiger territories. Fast urbanization, agrarian extension, and foundation improvement change once-wild scenes into human-ruled regions, passing on tigers with restricted space to meander. As normal prey turns out to be scant inside these divided living spaces, tigers might wander nearer to human settlements looking for food, setting off clashes an over area and assets.

The contracting cradle zones among woodlands and human homes heighten the possibilities of direct experiences. Tigers, frequently compelled to explore through human-ruled scenes, may wind up in nearness to towns and farming regions. This closeness expands the gamble of conflicts, with tigers going after domesticated animals or, in uncommon examples, representing a danger to living souls.

Retaliatory killings, a lamentable result of human-tiger clashes, further strain the sensitive concurrence. Because of seen dangers or genuine misfortunes of animals, networks might fall back on hurting or killing tigers. This not just represents an immediate danger to the generally imperiled tiger populaces yet in addition worsens the pattern of contention, making a hazardous criticism circle.

Tending to expanded human-tiger clashes requires a multi-layered approach that joins living space protection, local area commitment, and imaginative preservation systems. Laying out and keeping up with untamed life hallways to work with tiger development between divided environments can lessen the recurrence of experiences in human-overwhelmed regions. Training programs that bring issues to light about the significance of tigers in keeping up with natural equilibrium, combined with drives to remunerate networks for animals misfortunes, add to encouraging comprehension and resilience.

Protection endeavors should likewise zero in on practical land use arranging, adjusting the requirements of human advancement with the conservation of basic tiger living spaces. By exploring a way toward conjunction, where the two people and tigers can share the scene agreeably, we can moderate the heightening contentions and secure a future where these radiant hunters keep on wandering uninhibitedly in their normal territories. The test lies in finding a sensitive equilibrium that safeguards both human vocations and the significant biodiversity addressed by the notable tiger.

CHAPTER 4

Conservation Challenges

Protection, the honest stewardship of Earth's different environments and species, faces a variety of complicated difficulties in the advanced time. The sensitive harmony between human requirements and natural conservation is ceaselessly tried by elements, for example, living space corruption, environmental change, poaching, and the tireless extension of human exercises. In this investigation, we dive into the complex difficulties that preservation endeavors wrestle with, unwinding the complexities of safeguarding biodiversity in a consistently impacting world.

1. Environment Misfortune and Discontinuity:
   Maybe the most inescapable test facing preservation is the tenacious misfortune and discontinuity of normal living spaces. Urbanization, agribusiness, logging, and foundation improvement change once-flawless environments into divided patches, upsetting the interconnected trap of life. The results are desperate, as species subject to far reaching natural surroundings face decreased accessible space, elevated human-untamed life clashes, and expanded weakness to eradication. Protection systems should address natural surroundings safeguarding, reclamation, and the making of untamed life hallways to alleviate the effect of discontinuity.

2. Environmental Change:
   The ghost of environmental change creates a long shaded area over protection endeavors, modifying temperature designs, precipitation systems, and ocean levels. These movements force species to adjust or relocate to make due, provoking their capacity to adapt to fast ecological changes. Traditionalists wrestle with the requirement for versatile methodologies, including helped relocation, and the

advancement of strong environments fit for enduring the effects of environmental change.

3. Overexploitation and Poaching:

   The tireless quest for normal assets, energized by financial motivators and unlawful business sectors, puts tremendous tension on natural life populaces. Poaching for ivory, skins, body parts, and the overexploitation of fisheries imperil the endurance of various species. Protectionists go up against the complicated undertaking of carrying out powerful enemy of poaching measures, laying out safeguarded regions, and drawing in neighborhood networks to control the interest for unlawful natural life items.

4. Obtrusive Species:

   The presentation of non-local species, whether purposeful or incidental, represents an impressive test to local biodiversity. Obtrusive species can outcompete local widely varied vegetation, upset biological cycles, and adjust whole environments. Preservation endeavors include the recognizable proof and the executives of intrusive species, stressing anticipation and alleviation to shield the trustworthiness of regular living spaces.

5. Contamination and Pollution:

   The unavoidable impact of human exercises brings contaminations into air, water, and soil, unfavorably influencing biological systems and untamed life. Modern contaminations, agrarian overflow, plastic waste, and compound pollutants present direct dangers to biodiversity. Protection systems center around contamination anticipation, territory rebuilding, and backing for economical practices to address the main drivers of ecological defilement.

6. Illness Flare-ups:

   Arising irresistible illnesses, frequently exacerbated by human exercises and environmental change, present a developing danger to natural life populaces. Illnesses, for example, chytridiomycosis in creatures of land and water and white-nose disorder in bats can crush whole species. Preservationists wrestle with the requirement for checking, exploration, and measures to forestall the spread of illnesses inside weak populaces.

7. Human-Natural life Clashes:

   As human populaces extend and infringe into natural life environments, clashes among people and untamed life heighten. Crop assaulting, predation on domesticated animals, and periodic dangers to human wellbeing bring about retaliatory killings and stressed concurrence. Preservation challenges incorporate creating systems for alleviating clashes, carrying out local area based protection drives, and cultivating understanding among people and natural life.

8. Restricted Assets and Financing:
Protection endeavors frequently work in a climate of restricted assets and subsidizing. The immense size of biodiversity safeguarding requires critical monetary ventures, and contending needs might redirect consideration from protection drives. Traditionalists should explore the intricacies of getting financing, cultivating organizations, and pushing for the designation of assets to shield Earth's biodiversity.

9. Absence of Public Mindfulness and Commitment:
Protection challenges are intensified by an absence of far and wide open mindfulness and commitment. Figuring out the significance of biodiversity, the results of ecological corruption, and the job people play in protection is urgent. Moderates endeavor to overcome any barrier through instruction, effort, and backing to accumulate public help for manageable practices and approaches.

10. Political and Strategy Difficulties:
Protection endeavors are unpredictably attached to political will and strategy choices. Clashing interests, momentary financial gains, and changing political needs can impede viable preservation measures. Exploring the political scene requires a fragile harmony between preservation objectives and the more extensive financial and political setting.

11. Globalization and Exchange:
Globalization and worldwide exchange add to the spread of obtrusive species, the interest for untamed life items, and the double-dealing of normal assets. Preservation challenges incorporate tending to the natural effect of worldwide stockpile chains, upholding for manageable exchange rehearses, and teaming up on transboundary protection drives.

12. Innovative Progressions and Moral Worries:
While innovative progressions offer significant instruments for preservation, they additionally present moral difficulties. Issues like the utilization of robots for checking, hereditary designing for species protection, and the ramifications of cutting edge observation innovations raise moral contemplations that traditionalists should cautiously explore.

13. Aggregate and Intuitive Impacts:

Protection challenges seldom exist in segregation; rather, they frequently connect and intensify one another. The combined impacts of territory misfortune, environmental change, contamination, and different stressors provoke complex situations that interest incorporated and versatile protection procedures to at the same time address numerous difficulties.

Exploring the Way ahead:

Regardless of the considerable difficulties, protectionists and researchers stay committed to exploring the way ahead. Incorporated and versatile methodologies that embrace the intricacies of biological systems, connect with nearby networks, influence innovation mindfully, and encourage worldwide coordinated effort are fundamental.

Preservation achievement requires an aggregate obligation to protecting biodiversity, perceiving the interconnectedness of all life on The planet, and winding around a story where people and the regular world coincide agreeably.

In confronting the horde difficulties of protection, we set out on an excursion to get a manageable future — one where the rich embroidery of life keeps on prospering, environments flourish, and the sensitive equilibrium of biodiversity perseveres for a long time into the future.

4.1 Legal and illegal activities contributing to habitat loss

Natural surroundings misfortune, a basic driver of biodiversity decline, is energized by a horde of human exercises. While some are endorsed by regulation, others work in the shadows of lawlessness, by and large forming the direction of natural corruption. This investigation digs into the perplexing snare of legitimate and criminal operations that add to natural surroundings misfortune, taking apart the components, outcomes, and the basic for hearty preservation measures.

1. **Lawful Logging and Lumber Collecting:**
   Lawful logging, frequently did as a component of lumber reaping tasks, is a conspicuous supporter of living space misfortune around the world. As interest for wood items rises, both in homegrown development and global business sectors, immense breadths of timberlands capitulate to the trimming tool. While controlled logging practices might include replanting drives, the size of extraction frequently dominates the limit of environments to recover. Legitimate logging can prompt deforestation, upset natural life environments, and change the biological equilibrium of forested scenes.
2. **Rural Development and Land Transformation:**
   Rural development, a legitimate and inescapable practice, changes

different scenes into monoculture fields to satisfy the worldwide need for food and wares. Enormous scope getting free from regular living spaces for harvests, pastureland, and agribusiness exercises parts biological systems and speeds up environment misfortune. Legitimately endorsed land transformation adds to the deficiency of biodiversity, disturbs natural life relocation courses, and expands the weakness of local species to annihilation.

3. Foundation Advancement and Urbanization:
   Legitimate framework advancement and urbanization modify scenes to oblige developing human populaces. The development of streets, roadways, dams, and metropolitan regions frequently requires the getting free from normal natural surroundings. While these activities plan to address the issues of networks, the aggregate effect brings about territory fracture, loss of biodiversity, and the change of once-wild regions into human-ruled conditions.

4. Lawful Mining and Extractive Ventures:
   Extractive businesses, including digging for minerals, oil, and gas, work inside legitimate systems however leave an enduring engraving on regular territories. Open-pit mining, deforestation for asset extraction, and the going with framework can corrupt environments and add to territory misfortune. The extraction of minerals and petroleum derivatives has sweeping natural results, influencing soil quality, water frameworks, and the by and large environmental trustworthiness of scenes.

5. Legitimate Land-Use Changes:
   Legislatures, driven by monetary and advancement objectives, may establish legitimate land-use changes that influence regular living spaces. Drafting adjustments, changes in land residency frameworks, and the renaming of safeguarded regions can prompt territory misfortune and discontinuity. While these progressions might be planned to spike monetary development, the natural expenses can be significant, influencing both nearby and worldwide biodiversity.

6. Legitimate Water The executives and Dam Development:
   Water the board projects, including dam development and repository creation, frequently happen inside legitimate systems to meet water supply and energy needs. In any case, these tasks modify waterway environments, flood regular territories, and dislodge earthly and seagoing species. The lawful components of water the board projects feature the difficult compromises between addressing human necessities and moderating normal environments.

7. **Legitimate Land Infringement and Farming Extension:**
Legitimate land infringement, where farming exercises stretch out past assigned limits, adds to living space misfortune. The development of farmlands into safeguarded regions, wetlands, and other basic natural surroundings is in many cases worked with by legitimate or administrative escape clauses. This infringement disturbs environmental cycles, pieces scenes, and puts extra weight on weak biological systems.

8. **Unlawful Logging and Lumber Exchange:**
Working beyond legitimateness, unlawful logging and wood exchange address a huge threat to worldwide backwoods. Frequently connected with defilement, frail policing, unlawful organizations, unlawful logging prompts uncontrolled deforestation, loss of biodiversity, and debasement of biological systems. The undercover idea of this action makes it trying to control and represents an extreme danger to the trustworthiness of normal environments.

9. **Unlawful Horticultural Practices and Land Freedom:**
Wrongfully led agrarian practices, for example, cut and-consume cultivating and unregulated land freedom, add to broad natural surroundings misfortune. These exercises, frequently determined by resource horticulture or unlawful agribusiness activities, bring about the quick change of regular scenes into farmland. The illicitness of these practices worsens their ecological effect, prompting soil debasement, loss of biodiversity, and expanded weakness to fierce blazes.

10. **Untamed life Dealing and Poaching:**
Unlawful untamed life dealing and poaching, driven by interest for colorful pets, conventional meds, and creature parts, undermine various species and their territories. The unlawful exchange natural life disturbs biological systems by draining populaces of key species and modifying hunter prey elements. The illegal idea of this action presents difficulties for policing requires global collaboration to really battle.

11. **Land Getting and Unlawful Land Acquisitions:**
Land getting, the unlawful obtaining of land frequently through compulsion or defilement, brings about unapproved changes in land use. This unlawful practice uproots neighborhood networks, upsets customary land the executives practices, and prompts environment misfortune. Land snatching might be driven by speculative interests, agribusiness development, or framework projects directed without appropriate assent.

12. **Unlawful Mining and Asset Double-dealing:**
Illegal mining exercises, including distinctive and limited scope mining activities, add to environment misfortune in naturally delicate regions. The utilization of horrendous strategies, like mercury in gold mining, defiles water sources and debases scenes. The unregulated idea of unlawful mining intensifies ecological effects and postures difficulties for preservation endeavors.

13. **Impractical Fishing Practices:**
Unlawful, unreported, and unregulated (IUU) fishing rehearses add to natural surroundings debasement in marine and freshwater biological systems. Overfishing, disastrous fishing strategies, and bycatch frequently work outside legitimate systems, draining fish populaces and upsetting marine environments. Protection endeavors in this domain require more grounded guidelines, observing, and implementation to battle unreasonable fishing rehearses.

14. **Land Contamination and Unlawful Unloading:**
Unlawful unloading of waste, unsafe materials, and poisons represents an immediate danger to earthly and oceanic territories. Whether driven by unlawful garbage removal rehearses or the unapproved release of poisons, this action adds to soil debasement, water pollution, and territory misfortune. Legitimate systems should be supported to address the unlawful removal of waste and forestall natural corruption.

15. **Unlawful Urbanization and Settlements:**
The foundation of unlawful metropolitan settlements, frequently happening in biologically touchy regions, brings about natural surroundings misfortune and discontinuity. Fast and impromptu urbanization outside lawful systems prompts the getting free from normal scenes, expanded contamination, and the change of environments. Lawful systems for metropolitan preparation and drafting are basic to checking the extension of unlawful settlements.

16. **Native Land Privileges and Protection Clashes:**

Clashes between preservation endeavors and native land freedoms can add to territory misfortune. At the point when preservation drives encroach upon customary native domains without legitimate discussion and assent, it can prompt lawful debates and living space debasement. Finding some kind of harmony between protection objectives and regarding native land freedoms is fundamental for manageable and evenhanded preservation rehearses.

Tending to the Mind boggling Snare of Lawful and Criminal operations:

Preserving biodiversity despite territory misfortune requires a comprehensive and multi-pronged methodology. Lawful structures should be fortified and implemented to control exercises that add to environment debasement. Worldwide joint effort, straightforward administration, and local area commitment are fundamental parts of successful protection techniques. By tending to the underlying drivers of territory misfortune, carrying out feasible practices, and encouraging a common obligation to ecological stewardship, humankind can explore a way toward a future where biodiversity flourishes, environments prosper, and the fragile equilibrium of nature perseveres.

4.2Infrastructure development and its impact

Framework improvement is a sign of cultural advancement, molding the actual scene and giving the establishment to financial development. Notwithstanding, this quest for progression frequently comes at a huge expense for the climate. The development of streets, expressways, dams, metropolitan regions, and other foundation tasks can have extensive biological results, prompting environment misfortune, discontinuity, and modifications to regular biological systems. In this investigation, we dive into the multi-layered effect of framework improvement, looking at the natural difficulties, possible arrangements, and the basic for a reasonable methodology that orchestrates progress with ecological stewardship.

1. Natural surroundings Misfortune and Fracture:

   One of the essential ecological effects of foundation advancement is natural surroundings misfortune and discontinuity. The transformation of normal scenes into streets, structures, and different designs brings about the immediate annihilation of natural surroundings that help assorted greenery. This misfortune is especially critical in biologically delicate regions, like timberlands, wetlands, and waterfront districts. Moreover, the making of straight foundation, like streets and thruways, can section territories, disengaging populaces and obstructing the development of untamed life. Territory misfortune and discontinuity are perceived as significant supporters of biodiversity decline and represent a danger to the drawn out endurance of numerous species.

2. Adjusted Hydrological Examples:

   Foundation projects, particularly those including dams and supplies, can fundamentally change hydrological designs. Dams disturb regular stream, prompting changes in residue transport, supplement cycling, and the accessibility of water downstream. Adjusted hydrological systems can adversely influence amphibian environments, influencing fish movement, residue testimony, and the soundness of riparian natural surroundings. In seaside regions, foundation improvement might disturb normal flowing examples, prompting saltwater interruption and influencing the sensitive equilibrium of beach front biological systems.

3. Soil Disintegration and Corruption:
   The development of foundation frequently includes broad earth-moving exercises, prompting soil disintegration and corruption. Clearing land for improvement, particularly on slants, can open soil to disintegration by wind and water. Dregs spillover from building locales can bring about expanded turbidity in neighboring water bodies, adversely affecting sea-going biological systems.
   Soil debasement can likewise influence the richness of agrarian grounds adjoining foundation projects, prompting more extensive ecological and financial results.

4. Air and Water Contamination:
   Framework advancement can add to air and water contamination through the arrival of poisons from development exercises, vehicle discharges, and spillover from impenetrable surfaces. Building destinations might deliver dust, particulate matter, and contaminations out of sight, influencing air quality. Overflow from streets and metropolitan regions can convey poisons like weighty metals, oils, and synthetics into water bodies, prompting water contamination. These poisons present dangers to oceanic biological systems, human well-being, and the generally speaking ecological nature of the impacted regions.

5. Influence on Biodiversity:
   The change of normal territories and the fracture brought about by framework advancement can have serious ramifications for biodiversity. Species that rely upon explicit territories might confront populace declines or nearby terminations. Untamed life passages, fundamental for the development of species between divided natural surroundings, are frequently disturbed by streets and metropolitan turn of events, further secluding populaces. The deficiency of biodiversity reduces the environmental flexibility of biological systems as well as has flowing consequences for environment benefits that help human prosperity.

6. Environmental Change Effects:
   Foundation improvement can add to environmental change both

straightforwardly and in a roundabout way. The development and activity of framework frequently include the arrival of ozone depleting substance discharges, adding to an unnatural weather change. Also, changes in land utilize related with framework projects, like deforestation or modifications to wetlands, can affect carbon sequestration and further worsen environmental change. As the world wrestles with the difficulties of an evolving environment, economical framework rehearses are essential for relieving ecological effects.

7. **Uprooting of Networks:**
   Huge scope foundation undertakings can bring about the uprooting of nearby networks. The development of dams, thruways, and metropolitan regions might require the securing of land, prompting the movement of networks that have frequently lived as one with their regular environmental factors for ages. Constrained relocation can have social, social, and mental effects on networks, disturbing customary ways of life and making difficulties for local area prosperity.

8. **Clamor and Light Contamination:**

Metropolitan foundation advancement carries with it clamor and light contamination. The development and activity of streets, air terminals, and metropolitan regions produce clamor contamination, affecting both natural life and human wellbeing. Light contamination, brought about by the extreme and misled utilization of counterfeit light, can upset normal nighttime ways of behaving in creatures, influence biological systems, and add to energy squander.

Alleviation and Supportable Foundation Practices:
Perceiving the natural effects of foundation improvement, there is a developing accentuation on taking on feasible practices to moderate these impacts. The accompanying procedures are urgent for adjusting the basic for progress with natural stewardship:

1. **Key Preparation and Effect Appraisal:**
   Preceding the initiation of framework projects, extensive ecological effect evaluations (EIAs) ought to be led. These appraisals assess the likely natural results of an undertaking, recognizing ways of limiting and relieve adverse consequences. Key arranging that thinks about biological responsiveness, biodiversity areas of interest, and the network of regular territories is fundamental for limiting environment misfortune and fracture.

2. **Territory Protection and Rebuilding:**
   To counter the impacts of territory misfortune, foundation ventures

ought to integrate measures for natural surroundings protection and rebuilding. This might include making green spaces inside metropolitan regions, laying out untamed life halls to associate divided natural surroundings, and carrying out reforestation drives. Integrating regular elements into framework configuration can add to natural availability and the safeguarding of biodiversity.

3. **Green Foundation and Supportable Plan:**
   Green foundation rehearses include integrating regular components into the plan of metropolitan regions and framework projects. This might incorporate green rooftops, porous asphalts, and the protection of regular seepage designs. Supportable plan standards mean to decrease the biological impression of framework, upgrade biological system benefits, and make strong, harmless to the ecosystem spaces.

4. **Natural life Intersections and Passageways:**
   To address environment fracture brought about by streets and expressways, untamed life intersections and hallways can be integrated into framework arranging.
   These designs work with the protected development of natural life across streets, diminishing the gamble of impacts and supporting keeping up with hereditary variety inside populaces. Appropriate plan and execution of these highlights add to moderating the effect on untamed life environments.

5. **Reasonable Transportation Practices:**
   The transportation area, a significant supporter of foundation related natural effects, can take on maintainable practices. This incorporates advancing public transportation, creating green transportation advancements, and coordinating foundation with dynamic transportation modes like cycling and strolling. Maintainable transportation rehearses mean to lessen emanations, ease blockage, and limit the natural impression of movement.

6. **Wetland and Riparian Assurance:**
   Foundation projects close to wetlands, streams, and other riparian zones ought to integrate measures to safeguard these basic biological systems. Cushion zones, vegetative supports, and feasible stormwater the executives practices can forestall dregs overflow, lessen water contamination, and keep up with the soundness of oceanic natural surroundings. Safeguarding wetlands and riparian regions adds to in general biological system flexibility.

7. **Environment Versatile Foundation:**
   Despite environmental change, foundation activities ought to be

intended to be strong to the effects of outrageous climate occasions, rising ocean levels, and changing precipitation designs. Integrating environment strong highlights, like raised structures, practical waste frameworks, and versatile plan, assists foundation with enduring natural difficulties and adds to long haul supportability.

8. Local area Commitment and Social Contemplations:

The effective execution of supportable framework rehearses requires dynamic commitment with neighborhood networks. Including people group in dynamic cycles, addressing concerns connected with removal, and consolidating customary information add to socially comprehensive and naturally capable framework improvement. Local area commitment encourages a feeling of responsibility and guarantees that foundation projects line up with nearby requirements and values.

4.3Climate change exacerbating habitat fragmentation

Natural surroundings discontinuity, an outcome of human exercises modifying scenes, is currently additionally exacerbated by the unfurling emergency of environmental change. The mind boggling connection between these two peculiarities presents significant difficulties to biodiversity, biological systems, and the sensitive equilibrium of our planet. In this investigation, we unwind the manners by which environmental change heightens territory fracture, looking at the flowing impacts on natural life, biological systems, and the earnest requirement for versatile preservation methodologies.

1. Adjusted Temperature and Precipitation Examples:
   Environmental change appears through shifts in temperature and precipitation designs, affecting the circulation and construction of biological systems. As temperatures increase and precipitation designs become flighty, vegetation zones might move, prompting confuses between the scopes of plant and creature species. This adjustment in biological circumstances can bring about divided natural surroundings, compelling species to adjust or relocate to reasonable conditions, further adding to living space discontinuity.

2. Ocean Level Ascent and Seaside Natural surroundings Fracture:
   Increasing worldwide temperatures add to the softening of polar ice covers and glacial masses, prompting ocean level ascent. Beach front territories, including mangroves, estuaries, and wetlands, face the brunt of this change. As ocean levels infringe upon beach front regions, these fundamental living spaces shrivel and become divided. This fracture represents a serious danger to animal groups

reliant upon these waterfront biological systems, disturbing favorable places, relocation courses, and the complex equilibrium of biodiversity in these districts.

3. Expanded Recurrence and Force of Outrageous Occasions:
   Environmental change is related with an expansion in the recurrence and force of outrageous climate occasions, like tropical storms, out of control fires, floods, and dry seasons. These occasions can straightforwardly part living spaces by obliterating vegetation, modifying soil piece, and making actual hindrances to untamed life development. The repercussions of outrageous occasions frequently leaves scenes divided and powerless, making it trying for biological systems to recuperate and adjust.

4. Moving Untamed life Reaches and Passage Interruptions:
   Environment actuated changes in temperature and vegetation designs impact the scopes of natural life species. As species endeavor to follow reasonable environments, they might experience boundaries like metropolitan regions, horticulture, or foundation that disturb normal movement courses.
   Natural life passages, fundamental for keeping up with network between divided territories, may become lacking or non-useful because of the moving scopes of species, further secluding populaces.

5. Influence on Cornerstone Species and Trophic Fountains:
   Natural surroundings fracture exacerbated by environmental change can lopsidedly influence cornerstone species — species that assume a urgent part in keeping up with biological system design and capability. At the point when cornerstone species are divided or dislodged, it can set off trophic fountains, disturbing the equilibrium of hunter prey cooperations and changing the elements of whole biological systems. This outpouring impact has repercussions on biodiversity, environment versatility, and the administrations these biological systems give.

6. Changed Fire Systems and Living space Change:
   Changes in environment add to modified fire systems, affecting environments that are adjusted to explicit fire frequencies. Now and again, expanded temperatures and delayed dry seasons make conditions helpful for additional successive and extraordinary out of control fires. These fierce blazes can change scenes, part natural surroundings, and lead to the deficiency of plant and creature species that can't adapt to the fast changes in their current circumstance.

7. Sea Fermentation and Coral Reef Fracture:
   Environmental change stretches out its range to the seas, making

sea fermentation due the assimilation of abundance carbon dioxide. Coral reefs, basic marine territories, are especially defenseless. Increasing ocean temperatures and sea fermentation add to coral blanching and the breakdown of coral reef environments. As coral reefs decline, the territories they accommodate endless marine species become divided, affecting the perplexing snare of life in these submerged domains.

8. Interruption of Occasional Cycles and Movement:

Environmental change adjusts the timing and span of seasons, upsetting the occasional cycles that numerous species depend on for reproducing, relocation, and taking care of. Transient species, like birds and marine creatures, may confront difficulties in synchronizing their developments with changing ecological circumstances. This desynchronization can bring about divided movement courses, diminished accessibility of assets, and expanded weakness to dangers.

Alleviation and Versatile Preservation Methodologies:

Tending to the double difficulties of environment discontinuity and environmental change requires a diverse and versatile methodology. Protection procedures should include:

1. Environment Tough Territory Reclamation:
   Focusing on the rebuilding of debased environments and establishing environment strong scenes can improve the versatile limit of biological systems. This incorporates establishing local species that are versatile to environment stressors, reestablishing normal vegetation halls, and restoring regions impacted by outrageous occasions.

2. Planning Tough Natural life Passageways:
   Untamed life passages assume an essential part in moderating the effects of territory fracture. Planning versatile hallways that record for expected shifts in species ranges because of environmental change guarantees their adequacy. This might include key arrangement, environment availability appraisals, and nonstop checking to adjust to changing natural circumstances.

3. Safeguarded Region The executives and Development:
   Fortifying the administration of existing safeguarded regions and it is fundamental to extend their inclusion. Safeguarded regions act as shelters for biodiversity, giving asylums where species can adjust to evolving environments. Integrating environment flexibility into safeguarded region arranging guarantees their drawn out adequacy in protecting biological systems.

4. Manageable Land-Use Arranging:
   Taking on reasonable land-use arranging rehearses that record for
   environmental change is basic. This includes keeping away from the
   change of normal territories, safeguarding green spaces inside metropolitan regions, and incorporating environment contemplations into
   framework improvement to limit its effect on biological systems.
5. Worldwide Joint effort and Strategy Promotion:

Environmental change and living space discontinuity are worldwide difficulties that request global coordinated effort. Supporting for strategies
that focus on environment activity, territory protection, and maintainable improvement on a worldwide scale is pivotal. Composed endeavors among legislatures, non-administrative associations (NGOs), and the
confidential area are crucial for address the main drivers of these interconnected emergencies.

CHAPTER 5

Conservation Initiatives

Preservation drives structure the bedrock of endeavors to shield biodiversity, safeguard environments, and advance manageable concurrence among people and the normal world. Even with mounting natural difficulties, from living space misfortune to environmental change, a different exhibit of drives has arisen, driven by legislatures, non-legislative associations (NGOs), people group, and people. This investigation digs into the complex scene of protection drives, looking at their objectives, procedures, and the aggregate journey to save the extravagance of life on The planet.

1. Safeguarded Regions and Public Parks:
   One of the major mainstays of preservation drives is the foundation of safeguarded regions and public parks. These regions act as shelters for biodiversity, giving safe territories where widely varied vegetation can flourish without the prompt danger of living space obliteration or abuse. Legislatures overall assign and deal with these areas, utilizing procedures like drafting, guideline of human exercises, and natural life checking to guarantee the protection of biological systems and species.
2. Natural life Halls and Network:
   Perceiving the effect of living space fracture on biodiversity, preservation drives progressively center around making and keeping up with natural life passages. These passages work with the development of species between divided environments, fundamental for hereditary variety, movement, and keeping up with solid populaces. Traditionalists work to recognize key hallways, execute measures to

diminish obstructions, and guarantee safe entries for natural life across scenes modified by human exercises.

3. Territory Rebuilding and Recovery:

Environment rebuilding drives expect to turn around the effects of corruption and misfortune by effectively reestablishing regular biological systems. This might include reforestation endeavors, wetland rebuilding, and recovery of debased scenes. Progressives team up with neighborhood networks, using economical practices to improve the flexibility of environments and advance the recuperation of local species.

4. Supportable Land Use and Arranging:

Protection drives draw in with land-use wanting to advance supportability and equilibrium the necessities of human improvement with natural safeguarding.

This includes upholding for dependable practices in farming, ranger service, and metropolitan preparation. By incorporating preservation contemplations into land-use arrangements, drives mean to limit natural surroundings annihilation, safeguard indispensable environments, and encourage conjunction between human exercises and biodiversity.

5. Local area Based Preservation:

Engaging nearby networks is a vital feature of numerous protection drives. Local area based preservation perceives the fundamental job of networks in practical normal asset the executives. By including nearby occupants in dynamic cycles, carrying out preservation schooling programs, and making impetuses for mindful stewardship, these drives look to adjust protection objectives to the prosperity of networks.

6. Preservation Schooling and Effort:

Preservation drives grasp the meaning of public mindfulness and training in encouraging a culture of natural stewardship. Instructive projects and effort endeavors expect to advise the general population about the significance regarding biodiversity, biological systems, and the dangers they face. Through schools, local area studios, and computerized stages, these drives motivate a feeling of obligation and urge people to make a move on the side of protection objectives.

7. Reasonable The travel industry and Ecotourism:

The travel industry, when overseen reasonably, can add to protection endeavors. Feasible the travel industry drives center around limiting the natural effect of guest exercises, supporting nearby networks, and producing assets for protection projects. Ecotourism, specifically, underlines dependable travel rehearses that focus on ecological protection, nearby societies, and the prosperity of natural life.

8. **Species Preservation and Recuperation Projects:**
Numerous preservation drives target explicit species that are jeopardized, undermined, or needing recuperation. Species preservation programs include top to bottom examination, observing, and dynamic intercessions to safeguard and lift the populaces of designated species. Methods like hostage reproducing, territory reclamation, and hostile to poaching measures are utilized to guarantee the endurance and recuperation of these key species.

9. **Environmental Change Moderation and Variation:**
Addressing the effects of environmental change is essential to preservation drives. Methodologies center around both alleviation — diminishing ozone depleting substance outflows — and transformation — assisting environments and species with adapting to the evolving environment. Traditionalists team up with states, organizations, and networks to carry out feasible practices, advance environmentally friendly power, and foster strength procedures for biological systems confronting environment related difficulties.

10. **Hereditary Variety Preservation:**
Perceiving the significance of hereditary variety in guaranteeing the versatility and flexibility of species, preservation drives carry out hereditary protection programs. These projects might include the foundation of seed banks, safeguarding of hereditary material, and particular rearing projects to keep up with and improve the hereditary variety of compromised and imperiled species.

11. **Native and Conventional Information Joining:**
Native and nearby networks frequently have important conventional information about environments and economical asset the board. Protection drives progressively perceive the significance of coordinating this information into preservation rehearses. Cooperative organizations with native networks guarantee that protection endeavors regard customary practices, advance social safeguarding, and benefit from the insight went down through ages.

12. **Worldwide Cooperation and Arrangements:**
Preservation drives stretch out past public boundaries, with worldwide joint effort assuming a pivotal part in tending to worldwide natural difficulties. Peaceful accords and settlements, like the Show on Organic Variety (CBD) and the Ramsar Show on Wetlands, give structures to nations to cooperate on protection objectives. These

arrangements advance shared liability regarding safeguarding world-wide biodiversity and environments.

13. **Corporate and Confidential Area Commitment:**
The corporate and confidential areas are progressively becoming central members in preservation drives. Organizations are perceiving the significance of feasible practices, corporate social obligation, and interests in preservation projects. Associations between preservation associations and confidential elements add to financing, aptitude, and imaginative answers for protecting biodiversity.

14. **Innovation and Advancement in Protection:**
Mechanical headways assume a crucial part in current protection drives. Satellite imaging, drones, camera traps, and DNA investigation add to observing natural life, planning living spaces, and assembling critical information. Moderates influence innovation for research, against poaching endeavors, and public commitment, cultivating inventive answers for complex protection challenges.

15. **Promotion and Strategy Impact:**

Preservation drives effectively take part in promotion and strategy impact to shape regulation, guidelines, and worldwide structures that help ecological protection. Backing endeavors target issues, for example, deforestation, untamed life dealing, and environmental change, expecting to impact chiefs and prepare public help for compelling arrangements.

Difficulties and Future Bearings:

While protection drives have accomplished huge victories, they face various difficulties. Deficient subsidizing, political unresponsiveness, the fast speed of ecological debasement, and the interconnected idea of worldwide moves present impediments to protection endeavors. In any case, the developing scene of protection is set apart by flexibility, development, and a developing comprehension of the direness of our planetary emergency.

The eventual fate of protection will probably see an expanded accentuation on comprehensive, interdisciplinary methodologies that address the underlying drivers of ecological debasement. Overcoming any issues between preservation science, strategy, and public commitment will be vital. Coordinating native information, cultivating global cooperation, and saddling mechanical advancements will assume key parts in molding compelling preservation methodologies.

5.1 Existing conservation projects aimed at mitigating habitat fragmentation

Environment discontinuity represents an extreme danger to biodiversity, upsetting biological systems and endangering innumerable species, including charming ones like the Malayan tiger. Perceiving the desperation of this issue, protectionists and associations all over the planet have started different activities pointed toward relieving living space discontinuity. These activities take on different systems, including environment reclamation, hallway creation, local area commitment, and mechanical advancements to shield territories and advance species network.

2. The Significance of Passage Creation:

One successful methodology in alleviating environment fracture is the making of untamed life hallways. These pathways associate divided natural surroundings, permitting species to navigate scenes, keep up with hereditary variety, and access assets significant for their endurance. The Yellowstone to Yukon Preservation Drive (Y2Y) in North America embodies the progress of such undertakings. Y2Y centers around making a constant hallway traversing from Yellowstone Public Park in the U.S. to Canada's Yukon, working with the development of species like wild bears, wolves, and elk. This task underlines the meaning of transboundary joint effort and highlights how passages can act as life savers for species impacted by discontinuity.

3. Local area Based Preservation Drives:

Protection projects tending to living space discontinuity frequently perceive the urgent job of neighborhood networks in accomplishing economical arrangements. The Amazon Locale Safeguarded Regions (ARPA) program in Brazil embodies a local area based approach. ARPA connects with neighborhood networks in the preservation of basic environments, planning to safeguard tremendous region of the Amazon rainforest. By including native networks and offering help for manageable jobs, ARPA tends to territory fracture as well as supports a feeling of stewardship among those living in vicinity to crucial environments.

4. Territory Rebuilding for Network:

Reestablishing corrupted natural surroundings is one more fundamental part of alleviating territory fracture. The Incomparable Eastern Reaches Drive in Australia embodies this methodology, zeroing in on reconnecting divided environments along the eastern seaboard. By reestablishing debased scenes and making environmental halls, this drive means to upgrade network for local species, including the spotted-tail quoll and the strong owl. Natural surroundings rebuilding projects contribute not exclusively to the actual reconnection of scenes yet additionally to the restoration of environmental cycles essential for keeping up with sound biological systems.

5. Mechanical Advancements for Observing and The executives:

In the period of mechanical progression, preservation projects influence imaginative devices to screen and oversee living spaces. The Brilliant (Spatial Checking and Revealing Apparatus) innovation, generally utilized in enemy of poaching endeavors, embodies this pattern. Brilliant utilizes GPS and spatial planning to screen and track watching endeavors in safeguarded regions. By using innovation to battle criminal operations that add to natural surroundings discontinuity, projects like Brilliant upgrade the viability of preservation drives and add to the general prosperity of environments.

6. Worldwide Coordinated efforts for Cross-Boundary Protection:

Environment discontinuity frequently rises above political limits, requiring worldwide joint efforts to thoroughly resolve the issue. The European Green Belt drive epitomizes such cross-line collaboration. Extending from the Barents Ocean in the north to the Dark Ocean in the south, this drive means to make a natural hall, associating assorted environments across 24 nations. By encouraging cooperation on a mainland scale, the European Green Belt drive embodies the significance of global organizations in moderating territory fracture and advancing biodiversity preservation.

7. Private-Public Organizations:

Public-private organizations have arisen as important systems for financing and executing preservation projects. The Rainforest Establishment, working in the Congo Bowl, is a model of an organization that draws in nearby networks, legislatures, and confidential substances. By getting land privileges for native networks, the establishment tends to environment fracture and advances feasible land use rehearses. This model grandstands how cooperation among public and confidential elements can prompt creative, maintainable, and significant preservation results.

8. Preservation through Land Buy and Insurance:

Getting basic natural surroundings through land buy and security is an immediate and viable technique in relieving environment discontinuity. The Yellowstone to Yukon Protection Drive (Y2Y), referenced prior, includes the procurement of key bundles of land to make a constant passage. Additionally, the Nature Conservancy's endeavors in the Appalachians center around purchasing and safeguarding area to associate divided living spaces. These drives underline the significance of key land preservation in guaranteeing the drawn out reasonability of environments and the species they support.

9. Difficulties and Illustrations Learned:

Regardless of the triumphs of different preservation projects, challenges continue in the relief of territory discontinuity. These difficulties incorporate asset requirements, contending land-use interests, and the complicated transaction of financial variables. Illustrations gained from these ventures highlight the significance of versatile administration, local area commitment, and interdisciplinary joint effort. Perceiving that protection is a dynamic and developing field, effective ventures ceaselessly adjust their procedures in light of new bits of knowledge and evolving conditions.

10. Future Headings and Worldwide Goals:

Looking forward, the relief of living space discontinuity requests a worldwide responsibility and facilitated endeavors. Protection activities ought to embrace innovative headways, integrate the bits of knowledge of nearby networks, and focus on the making of interconnected scenes. Worldwide goals, for example, environmental change further highlight the earnestness of tending to natural surroundings discontinuity, as interconnected territories improve species' flexibility to ecological movements.

5.2Success stories and lessons learned

Preservation endeavors across the globe have yielded striking examples of overcoming adversity, exhibiting the potential for positive effect when networks, associations, and state run administrations join to safeguard biodiversity. These examples of overcoming adversity celebrate accomplishments as well as give significant illustrations to future undertakings in shielding the planet's biological systems.

**1. The Recuperation of the Bald Eagle:

The recuperation of the bald eagle in the US remains as a demonstration of the viability of designated preservation endeavors. During the twentieth hundred years, boundless pesticide use, especially DDT, prompted a sharp decrease in bald eagle populaces because of eggshell diminishing and conceptive disappointments. Perceiving the approaching danger, the U.S. government restricted DDT in 1972 and carried out preservation measures, including environment security and hostage rearing projects.

The example of overcoming adversity of the bald eagle outlines the significance of quick administrative activity and cooperative preservation drives. The execution of legitimate measures, joined with territory rebuilding and public mindfulness crusades, prompted the expulsion of the bald eagle from the jeopardized species list in 2007. This achievement highlights the strength of species when given a favorable climate for recuperation.

**2. The Protection of Monster Pandas:

The protection excursion of monster pandas in China fills in as a notable illustration of global coordinated effort and all encompassing preservation techniques. Confronting living space misfortune and fracture, combined with low regenerative rates, goliath pandas were near the very edge of termination. China's endeavors to lay out safeguarded stores and hallways for pandas, alongside global coordinated efforts and public commitment, have added to a momentous circle back.

Progress in monster panda protection features the significance of long haul responsibility, including neighborhood networks, and tending to main drivers like environment misfortune.

By coordinating logical exploration, territory security, and local area contribution, the preservation endeavors for goliath pandas have turned into a model for protecting leader species and their biological systems.

**3. The Restoration of the Iberian Lynx:

The Iberian lynx, one of the world's most jeopardized cat species, confronted a basic decay because of living space misfortune, discontinuity, and a decline in its principal prey, the European bunny. Preservationists in Spain and Portugal attempted an aggressive recuperation plan, tending to territory reclamation, hostage reproducing, and prey the executives.

The fruitful recuperation of the Iberian lynx highlights the significance of versatile administration and logical examination. Progressives firmly observed lynx populaces, changed methodologies in light of new information, and drew in neighborhood networks in the recuperation endeavors. The Iberian lynx story underscores the requirement for dynamic preservation moves toward that advance with the changing necessities of species and biological systems.

**4. The Coral Reefs of Palau:

Palau, an archipelago in the western Pacific, has shown progress in marine preservation by laying out one of the world's most memorable shark asylums and executing measures to safeguard coral reefs. Palau perceived the biological significance of sharks and the job they play in keeping up with the equilibrium of marine environments. By assigning its waters as a safe-haven, Palau has started a trend for shark protection and marine biodiversity conservation.

The Palauan example of overcoming adversity features the meaning of local area driven protection and the joining of conventional environmental information. In Palau, the foundation of marine safeguarded regions included coordinated effort with neighborhood networks and regard for native practices. This approach encourages a feeling of pride and obligation, basic components in the economical administration of regular assets.

**5. The Rebound of the California Condor:

The California condor looked close termination in the late twentieth hundred years because of lead harming from ingesting spent lead ammo and environment debasement. Preservationists set out on a concentrated hostage reproducing system to increment condor numbers and carried out lead reduction measures.

The recuperation of the California condor epitomizes the viability of composed reproducing programs and designated mediations.

By tending to explicit dangers and consolidating hostage rearing with natural surroundings insurance, the California condor populace has encountered an outstanding resurgence. The condor's story highlights the significance of tending to numerous aspects of protection all the while.

Illustrations Learned:

While praising these examples of overcoming adversity, a few key illustrations have arisen that can direct future preservation endeavors:

**1. Comprehensive Protection Approaches:

Effective protection frequently requires a far reaching, all encompassing methodology that tends to different parts of an animal varieties' nature and dangers to its endurance. Joining natural surroundings reclamation, hostage reproducing, lawful insurance, and local area commitment frames a vigorous procedure that improves the probability of progress.

**2. Versatile Administration:

Protection endeavors should be versatile and receptive to new data and evolving conditions. Customary checking and assessment of protection programs empower specialists to change methodologies, consolidating the most recent logical bits of knowledge and answering arising difficulties.

**3. Local area Commitment and Instruction:

Including nearby networks in preservation drives is critical for long haul achievement. Local area commitment cultivates a feeling of stewardship, adjusts preservation endeavors to neighborhood needs, and can give important bits of knowledge into biological elements.

**4. Global Cooperation:

Protection challenges frequently rise above public boundaries, requiring worldwide collaboration. Effective preservation projects influence worldwide coordinated efforts, share information, and pool assets to address the interconnected difficulties looked by biodiversity.

**5. Regulation and Strategy Backing:

The establishment and requirement of viable preservation regulation assume a urgent part in safeguarding species and their territories. The examples of overcoming adversity referenced feature the significance of administrative measures that restrict destructive exercises and advance living space conservation.

**6. Public Mindfulness and Promotion:

Public mindfulness and promotion endeavors are fundamental for gathering backing and encouraging a protection disapproved of ethos. Examples of overcoming adversity frequently include public missions that bring issues to light, form support, and add to positive protection results.

**7. Interest in Logical Exploration:

Logical exploration frames the groundwork of successful preservation. Figuring out the biological necessities of species, checking populace elements, and exploring the effects of dangers are essential to creating proof based preservation techniques.

**8. Feasible Practices:

Protection projects that consolidate feasible practices, whether in natural surroundings rebuilding or local area commitment, add to the drawn out practicality of biological systems. Offsetting preservation objectives with maintainable improvement guarantees the all around was of both regular and human networks.

5.3 The role of international collaboration in tiger conservation

Worldwide coordinated effort assumes an essential part in tiger protection, as the preservation of these glorious animals stretches out past public boundaries. Tigers, confronting dangers like environment misfortune, poaching, and human-untamed life struggle, require coordinated endeavors on a worldwide scale to guarantee their endurance.

One remarkable illustration of worldwide coordinated effort in tiger protection is the Worldwide Tiger Drive (GTI). Sent off in 2010 by the World Bank, in association with nations holding onto wild tiger populaces, the GTI plans to twofold the quantity of wild tigers by 2022 - the Extended time of the Tiger in the Chinese zodiac. This aggressive drive perceives that the endurance of tigers requires composed activity among tiger-range nations, worldwide associations, and the worldwide local area.

The GTI centers around key mainstays of tiger preservation, including living space security, hostile to poaching endeavors, and local area commitment. By encouraging joint effort among nations like India, Russia, Indonesia, and others, the GTI works with the sharing of best practices, logical examination, and assets. This cooperative methodology upgrades the adequacy of preservation procedures, guaranteeing that endeavors are synchronized and lined up with the natural necessities of tiger populaces.

Moreover, global associations, for example, the Show on Worldwide Exchange Imperiled Types of Wild Fauna and Greenery (Refers to) assume a urgent part in controlling and checking the worldwide exchange of tiger parts. The joint effort worked with by Refers to fortifies the requirement of guidelines pointed toward checking unlawful dealing and poaching of tigers.

CHAPTER 6

Technological Solutions

In the high speed scene of the 21st hundred years, innovation remains as a guide of development, offering answers for complex difficulties across different spaces. From medical services to natural preservation, training to correspondence, mechanical progressions have the ability to change social orders and reshape the manner in which we explore the world. This investigation dives into the complex domain of innovative arrangements, looking at their effect, potential, and the moral contemplations that go with their incorporation into our day to day routines.

1. Medical care Transformation:
   Mechanical developments have upset medical services, improving diagnostics, therapy, and generally speaking patient consideration. Telemedicine, for example, empowers distant meetings, giving admittance to clinical skill paying little heed to geographic requirements. Wearable gadgets outfitted with wellbeing checking sensors permit people to follow indispensable signs, encouraging preventive consideration. Computerized reasoning (computer based intelligence) aids clinical imaging investigation, accelerating determination and further developing exactness. The reconciliation of innovation further develops medical care proficiency as well as democratizes access, connecting holes in clinical benefits worldwide.
2. Schooling Innovation (EdTech):
   EdTech has changed conventional schooling ideal models, offering intelligent and customized opportunities for growth. Virtual study halls and online stages empower schooling access independent of actual limits. Versatile learning frameworks use simulated intelligence to fit instructive substance to individual requirements, upgrading

cognizance and maintenance. Gamification draws in understudies through intelligent and vivid encounters. The joining of innovation in training reaches out past proper settings, supporting long lasting mastering and expertise improvement, making a more comprehensive and dynamic learning climate.

3. Correspondence Development:

The development of correspondence advances has significantly influenced the manner in which people associate and offer data. Virtual entertainment stages work with worldwide correspondence, encouraging associations and data dispersal. Informing applications, video conferencing devices, and cooperative stages span distances, empowering continuous connection.

The appearance of 5G innovation guarantees quicker and more dependable network, further changing the scene of correspondence. Notwithstanding, moral contemplations encompassing security, falsehood, and computerized separates require smart route of this mechanical outskirts.

4. Maintainable Horticulture and Accuracy Cultivating:

Notwithstanding worldwide food security challenges, innovation assumes a critical part in molding economical farming practices. Accuracy cultivating utilizes sensors, robots, and information investigation to enhance crop the executives, lessen asset use, and limit natural effect. Brilliant cultivating advances empower ongoing observing of soil wellbeing, weather patterns, and yield development. Mechanical technology and computerization add to errands like planting and collecting, expanding effectiveness. The combination of horticulture and innovation holds guarantee in guaranteeing food creation satisfies the needs of a developing worldwide populace while limiting natural impressions.

5. Sustainable power Arrangements:

Mechanical developments in the domain of environmentally friendly power have arisen as essential parts in addressing environmental change and progressing to manageable energy sources. Sun oriented and wind energy innovations keep on progressing, turning out to be more productive and financially savvy. Energy capacity arrangements, like high level batteries, alleviate the irregular idea of inexhaustible sources. Brilliant lattices streamline energy circulation, upgrading strength and unwavering quality. The combination of innovation in the energy area is fundamental to accomplishing a cleaner, more practical future and decreasing reliance on petroleum derivatives.

6. Natural Observing and Protection:
   In the domain of natural protection, innovation offers key apparatuses for observing and defending biological systems. Satellite symbolism and remote detecting empower ongoing following of deforestation, biodiversity misfortune, and environmental change influences. Sensor organizations and Web of Things (IoT) gadgets gather information on natural factors, helping with environment protection endeavors. Computer based intelligence calculations investigate immense datasets, distinguishing designs and foreseeing natural patterns. Innovation not just works with a more profound comprehension of environmental frameworks yet in addition enables protectionists to carry out designated techniques for saving biodiversity.

7. Metropolitan Preparation and Brilliant Urban areas:
   The idea of brilliant urban areas use innovation to improve metropolitan living, maintainability, and proficiency. IoT gadgets, sensors, and information investigation streamline asset the executives, transportation frameworks, and foundation. Shrewd networks further develop energy circulation, diminishing waste. Insightful transportation frameworks ease gridlock and improve public travel. Innovation additionally cultivates resident commitment through computerized stages, empowering participatory metropolitan preparation. While the vision of shrewd urban communities holds guarantee for upgraded personal satisfaction, moral contemplations incorporate information protection, security, and impartial admittance to mechanical advantages.

8. Mechanical technology and Robotization:
   Progressions in advanced mechanics and computerization have groundbreaking ramifications across different enterprises. In assembling, robots smooth out creation processes, expanding productivity and accuracy. In medical care, mechanical helped medical procedures improve careful capacities. Independent vehicles, including robots and self-driving vehicles, alter transportation and strategies. While these advancements offer various benefits, moral contemplations like work uprooting, wellbeing, and mindful man-made intelligence improvement require cautious consideration in their execution.

9. Space Investigation and Colonization:
   The investigation of room has entered another period with innovative headways empowering aggressive missions and the possibility of human colonization past Earth. Space telescopes give uncommon perspectives on far off worlds, growing comprehension we might

interpret the universe. Confidential space organizations are creating reusable rocket innovation, bringing down the expense of room travel. While the fantasy about colonizing different planets presents invigorating conceivable outcomes, moral contemplations incorporate planetary insurance, asset use, and the likely effect on extraterrestrial conditions.

10. Man-made reasoning and AI:

Man-made brainpower (artificial intelligence) and AI (ML) advances are at the very front of extraordinary development. Artificial intelligence applications range from normal language handling and picture acknowledgment to prescient investigation and independent frameworks. AI calculations break down tremendous datasets, uncovering examples and making forecasts. While man-made intelligence holds enormous potential, moral contemplations with respect to predisposition, responsibility, and the cultural effect of mechanization require continuous investigation and dependable turn of events.

11. Network safety Arrangements:

As our dependence on innovation develops, so does the significance of network safety answers for safeguard against advanced dangers. Encryption advances protect delicate information, guaranteeing protection and secure interchanges. Computer based intelligence fueled online protection devices break down network traffic examples to identify abnormalities and potential digital assaults. The persistent advancement of online protection measures is basic in alleviating the dangers related with an interconnected computerized scene.

12. Customized Medication and Genomics:

Mechanical headways in genomics and customized medication are reshaping medical services by fitting therapies to individual hereditary profiles. Cutting edge sequencing advances empower the unraveling of whole genomes, giving bits of knowledge into hereditary inclinations and customized treatment choices. Accuracy medication thinks about individual varieties in qualities, way of life, and climate for more compelling medical services mediations. Moral contemplations incorporate protection concerns connected with hereditary information and evenhanded admittance to arising clinical advancements.

Challenges and Moral Contemplations:

As we embrace innovative answers for address heap difficulties, moral contemplations become fundamental. Key difficulties and moral aspects include:

Protection Concerns:

The assortment and use of tremendous measures of individual information raise worries about security. Finding some kind of harmony between mechanical headways and individual security privileges requires strong lawful systems and moral rules.

Value and Access:

The advanced separation worsens social imbalances, with abberations in admittance to innovation and its advantages. Guaranteeing impartial admittance to innovative arrangements is fundamental for forestalling the further underestimation of underserved networks.

Work Dislodging and Monetary Movements:

Computerization and mechanical technology might prompt work removal in specific businesses. Tending to the financial movements related with innovative progressions requires proactive measures, for example, retraining projects and approaches supporting the change to new work open doors.

Moral man-made intelligence and Predisposition:

The turn of events and organization of simulated intelligence frameworks raise worries about inclination, responsibility, and straightforwardness. Guaranteeing that simulated intelligence calculations are fair, unprejudiced, and responsible requires moral rules, progressing investigation, and capable man-made intelligence improvement rehearses.

Natural Effect:

The creation and removal of electronic gadgets add to natural corruption. Maintainable innovation works on, including reusing drives and eco-accommodating plan standards, are pivotal for limiting the natural effect of mechanical arrangements.

Security Dangers:

The interconnected idea of advanced frameworks presents security gambles, including digital assaults and information breaks. Reinforcing network safety measures and cultivating a culture of computerized education are fundamental for defending people, associations, and basic framework.

6.1 Use of technology in monitoring and managing tiger habitats

In the journey to moderate and safeguard imperiled species like the tiger, innovation arises as a strong partner, upsetting the manner in which we screen and deal with their living spaces. Quick progressions in remote detecting, information examination, and network have introduced another time of protection, where state of the art devices offer exceptional bits of knowledge into the elements of tiger territories. This investigation digs into the imaginative utilization of innovation in observing and overseeing tiger environments, analyzing the apparatuses, procedures, and the extraordinary effect on protection endeavors.

1. **Satellite Innovation for Natural surroundings Planning:**
   Satellite innovation has turned into a foundation in observing tiger natural surroundings according to a worldwide viewpoint. High-goal satellite symbolism gives nitty gritty guides of land cover, vegetation, and changes in land use. These guides help protectionists in distinguishing reasonable environments, checking deforestation or infringement, and surveying the general soundness of tiger scenes. The capacity to accumulate extensive information from space works with informed decision-production for environment assurance and rebuilding drives.

2. **GIS and Spatial Investigation:**
   Geographic Data Frameworks (GIS) and spatial investigation apparatuses add to the accuracy and profundity of territory checking. By incorporating satellite symbolism with spatial information, moderates can make point by point natural surroundings maps, recognize passages, and survey the availability of scenes. GIS innovation empowers the displaying of environment appropriateness, focusing on regions for preservation mediations in light of biological importance and the potential for tiger presence.

3. **Camera Snares for Natural life Checking:**
   Camera traps have changed natural life checking, offering a nonnosy and proficient strategy for concentrating on tiger populaces. Furnished with movement sensors, these cameras catch pictures or recordings when set off by the development of creatures. Traditionalists send camera traps decisively in tiger natural surroundings to assess populace sizes, screen conduct, and track individual tigers. The information gathered supports grasping populace elements, recognizing dangers, and planning designated preservation procedures.

4. **DNA Investigation for Populace Hereditary qualities:**
   DNA investigation has arisen as a significant device for figuring out the hereditary wellbeing and variety of tiger populaces. Painless examining, like gathering scat or hair from tigers in the wild, gives hereditary material to examination. Preservation geneticists utilize this information to survey hereditary variety, recognize family connections, and identify possible inbreeding. Such bits of knowledge illuminate protection procedures pointed toward safeguarding the drawn out suitability of tiger populaces.

5. Remote Detecting and Deforestation Observing:
Remote detecting advances, including LiDAR (Light Discovery and Going) and RADAR (Radio Identification and Running), are instrumental in checking deforestation and natural surroundings misfortune. LiDAR, for example, can infiltrate thick vegetation to give definite 3D planning of backwoods structure.
Progressives utilize these advances to identify changes in woods cover, survey the effect of logging or land clearing, and focus on regions for living space reclamation.

6. Brilliant Innovation for Against Poaching Endeavors:
Spatial Checking and Detailing Device (Brilliant) innovation is a far reaching device utilized in the battle against poaching. Coordinating GPS, spatial planning, and information examination, Shrewd empowers constant observing of watching endeavors in tiger natural surroundings. Park officers furnished with GPS-empowered gadgets can record their developments, report episodes of criminal operations, and add to a concentrated framework for following and answering expected dangers.

7. Acoustic Observing for Vocalizations:
Acoustic observing uses sound-recording gadgets decisively positioned in tiger natural surroundings to catch vocalizations, including thunders, snarls, and other correspondence signals. These accounts give significant experiences into tiger presence, conduct, and region elements. Acoustic information, joined with other checking strategies, upgrades how we might interpret the social design and conceptive exercises of tiger populaces.

8. Drones for Ethereal Reviews:
Automated Ethereal Vehicles (UAVs), or drones, offer an elevated perspective of tiger environments, working with flying reviews and checking. Drones outfitted with cameras or sensors can cover huge regions rapidly and catch high-goal symbolism. Moderates use robots to evaluate living space conditions, recognize criminal operations, and guide scenes with a degree of detail that was formerly difficult to accomplish.

9. Information Investigation and AI:
The tremendous measures of information produced by different observing advancements are saddled through information investigation and AI calculations. These high level scientific devices process information to recognize designs, foresee environment changes, and even computerize the order of satellite symbolism. AI models can help with recognizing possible dangers, like infringement or natural

surroundings debasement, considering proactive preservation measures.

10. **Availability and Sensor Organizations:**
    The Web of Things (IoT) and sensor networks add to ongoing observing of tiger environments. Sending sensors in key areas considers persistent information assortment on variables like temperature, mugginess, and creature development.
    Availability empowers the transmission of this information to incorporated frameworks, furnishing protectionists with modern data on natural circumstances and possible unsettling influences.

11. **Warm Imaging for Nighttime Checking:**
    Warm imaging innovation empowers checking of tiger living spaces during nighttime hours when numerous creatures, including tigers, are dynamic. Warm cameras can distinguish heat marks, permitting scientists to follow the development of creatures in complete murkiness. This innovation upgrades the precision of populace gauges and social examinations, adding to a more far reaching comprehension of tiger biology.

12. **Resident Science and Portable Applications:**
    Connecting with the general population in protection endeavors is worked with through resident science drives and portable applications. Preservation associations create applications that permit clients to contribute significant information, like tiger sightings or indications of criminal operations. Resident science drives influence the force of a worldwide local area to improve observing endeavors, growing the scope of protection drives past conventional limits.

13. **Computer generated Reality (VR) and Expanded Reality (AR):**

Computer generated Reality (VR) and Expanded Reality (AR) advancements offer vivid encounters that guide in protection training and public mindfulness. VR recreations can ship clients into tiger living spaces, encouraging a more profound association with these environments. AR applications empower clients to overlay data about tiger protection on genuine conditions, making intelligent and instructive encounters.

Difficulties and Future Bearings:
While the utilization of innovation in observing and overseeing tiger living spaces has exhibited huge victories, a few difficulties endure:

Cost and Openness:
The underlying venture and progressing costs related with cutting edge innovations can be restrictive. Guaranteeing openness to these devices

for moderates and associations working in asset compelled districts stays a test.

Information Reconciliation and Normalization:

The reconciliation of information from numerous sources, for example, satellite symbolism, camera traps, and acoustic checking, requires normalized conventions and interoperability. Creating normal systems for information sharing and examination is urgent for boosting the adequacy of innovation driven preservation endeavors.

Moral Contemplations:

The utilization of innovation raises moral contemplations connected with protection, information possession, and likely disturbances to regular ways of behaving. Finding some kind of harmony between compelling observing and regarding the independence of untamed life is fundamental.

Limit Building and Preparing:

Progressives and nearby networks need satisfactory preparation to tackle the maximum capacity of innovative devices. Building limit and guaranteeing that clients are capable in using these advances are basic parts of fruitful execution.

Network protection Concerns:

As protection drives become more dependent on computerized advancements and network, the gamble of online protection dangers increments. Safeguarding touchy information and guaranteeing the solid effort of innovation based frameworks are vital contemplations.

Variation to Quick Natural Changes:

The speed of natural change, driven by variables, for example, environmental change and living space corruption, requires advancements that can adjust rapidly. Creating versatile observing methodologies that stay up with dynamic environments is a continuous test.

Local area Commitment and Social Acknowledgment:

Bringing innovation into neighborhood networks might confront difficulties connected with social acknowledgment and social contemplations. Compelling people group commitment techniques are fundamental to guarantee that innovation is embraced as a device for protection.

Proceeded with Development:

The area of innovation is dynamic, with constant headways and new instruments arising. Remaining at the front line of mechanical advancement and incorporating new devices into preservation procedures is urgent for guaranteeing the significance and viability of checking endeavors.

In exploring these difficulties, the future bearings of innovation in observing and overseeing tiger environments are set apart by progressing development and coordinated effort. Key contemplations include:

Cooperative Innovative work:

Joint efforts between protection associations, tech organizations, research establishments, and neighborhood networks can drive the improvement of custom fitted mechanical arrangements. Innovative work drives that focus on coordinated effort work with the formation of setting explicit devices that address the special difficulties of tiger protection.

Open Information Stages and Resident Commitment:

Laying out open information stages and empowering resident commitment add to straightforwardness, responsibility, and a more extensive information pool. Engaging residents to partake in checking endeavors improves the compass and effect of preservation drives, cultivating a feeling of shared liability.

Reconciliation of Man-made reasoning (simulated intelligence):

The reconciliation of man-made reasoning, including AI and PC vision, holds guarantee for robotizing information investigation and understanding. Man-made intelligence calculations can process tremendous datasets all the more proficiently, permitting progressives to zero in on essential navigation and protection arranging.

Adaptable Innovation Arrangements:

Perceiving the variety of territories and protection challenges, adjustable innovation arrangements that can be adjusted to explicit settings are fundamental. Fitting innovation to the requirements of various areas and biological systems guarantees importance and adequacy in differed protection situations.

Limit Building and Preparing Projects:

Putting resources into limit building and preparing programs is urgent for guaranteeing that protection experts, neighborhood networks, and pertinent partners have the right stuff expected to successfully use innovation. Preparing projects ought to include the activity of innovation as well as moral contemplations and best practices.

Strategy Backing and Administrative Structures:

Policymakers assume a significant part in supporting the mix of innovation into preservation endeavors. Laying out administrative structures, boosting the utilization of innovation for preservation, and cultivating a strong strategy climate add to the fruitful reception of mechanical instruments.

Long haul Checking and Versatile Administration:

Executing long haul checking programs and versatile administration systems guarantees the proceeded with importance of innovation driven preservation drives. Ordinary appraisals of the adequacy of observing instruments, combined with adaptability to adjust to evolving conditions, are fundamental parts of fruitful protection endeavors.

6.2 GIS and remote sensing applications in conservation

Geographic Data Frameworks (GIS) and remote detecting advancements have arisen as essential apparatuses in the field of preservation, reforming the manner in which we grasp, screen, and oversee regular biological systems. These strong innovations give a spatial point of view that rises above customary information investigation techniques, offering preservationists an exhaustive perspective on scenes, biodiversity, and ecological changes. This investigation digs into the utilizations of GIS and remote detecting in protection, featuring their groundbreaking effect on natural stewardship.

1. Planning Biodiversity and Biological systems:

   One of the principal uses of GIS in preservation is the planning of biodiversity and environments. GIS permits moderates to make itemized maps that exhibit the circulation of species, living spaces, and biological elements. By overlaying different layers of spatial information, for example, vegetation types, geography, and environment, GIS works with the recognizable proof of biodiversity areas of interest, basic living spaces, and areas of biological importance. These guides act as significant instruments for preservation arranging, focusing on regions for security and rebuilding endeavors.

2. Natural surroundings Appropriateness Displaying:

   GIS assumes a crucial part in living space reasonableness displaying, a cycle that predicts the most appropriate territories for explicit species. By incorporating natural factors, like temperature, precipitation, and land cover, GIS models can gauge the appropriateness of various regions for the endurance and propagation of target species. Protectionists utilize these models to distinguish expected natural surroundings for renewed introduction programs, survey the effect of environmental change on species circulations, and illuminate land-use intending to limit living space misfortune.

3. Preservation Arranging and Land Use The executives:

   GIS works with protection arranging by giving a spatial structure to independent direction. Moderates use GIS to dissect scenes, survey the effect of human exercises, and configuration safeguarded regions or natural life hallways. Land use the executives methodologies

benefit from GIS-based examinations that consider factors like availability, fracture, and the natural necessities of species.

The mix of spatial information guarantees that preservation arranging lines up with the more extensive objectives of manageable
land use.

4. Observing and Relief of Deforestation:

Remote detecting advances, combined with GIS, empower the observing and alleviation of deforestation — an intense danger to biodiversity. Satellite symbolism catches changes in backwoods cover
over the long run, permitting progressives to distinguish deforestation areas of interest, evaluate the degree of timberland misfortune,
and recognize regions in bad shape. GIS apparatuses help in planning
methodologies to relieve deforestation, for example, reforestation
programs, and add to the requirement of protection strategies by
giving proof of unlawful logging exercises.

5. Untamed life Populace Checking:

GIS and remote detecting advances, including satellite symbolism
and ethereal reviews, add to the checking of untamed life populaces.
Moderates use GIS to plan and enhance the situation of camera
traps, which catch pictures of creatures in their normal territories. Remote detecting information improve populace gauges, track
movement examples, and screen changes in the overflow and dispersion of species. This data is vital for grasping populace elements,
surveying the progress of protection mediations, and distinguishing
expected dangers.

6. Environmental Change Effect Evaluation:

Environmental change presents critical difficulties to biological systems and biodiversity. GIS and remote detecting give fundamental
devices to surveying the effect of environmental change on normal
natural surroundings. These advances assist with demonstrating
changes in temperature, precipitation, and other climatic factors,
permitting traditionalists to foresee how species conveyances might
move over the long haul. By understanding the possible impacts of
environmental change, protection endeavors can be custom fitted
to improve the strength of biological systems and species.

7. Wetland and Water Asset The board:

GIS is instrumental in wetland and water asset the board, supporting
protection endeavors in basic oceanic environments. Remote detecting information can be utilized to screen changes in wetland degree,
water quality, and the wellbeing of amphibian living spaces. GIS
apparatuses help in the recognizable proof of wetland preservation

needs, the appraisal of human effects on water assets, and the plan of methodologies to secure and reestablish sea-going environments.

8. Intrusive Species Checking and The board:
   Intrusive species represent a huge danger to local biodiversity. GIS works with the checking and the board of intrusive species by giving instruments to planning their dispersion, grasping their spread examples, and surveying the environmental effects. Remote detecting information add to the ID of regions attacked by non-local species, empowering fast reaction procedures to control and relieve their effect on nearby biological systems.

9. Infection Observation and Preservation Wellbeing:
   GIS applications stretch out to sickness observation in natural life populaces. By planning the appropriation of natural life infections, traditionalists can distinguish illness areas of interest, screen the spread of microbes, and execute designated mediations.
   GIS upholds the mix of wellbeing information with spatial data, taking into consideration a thorough comprehension of the cooperations between natural life wellbeing, territory conditions, and ecological elements.

10. Marine and Coral Reef Preservation:

GIS and remote detecting advancements are fundamental for marine and coral reef preservation. Satellite symbolism gives a perspective on marine environments, taking into consideration the checking of coral reef wellbeing, ocean surface temperatures, and the effect of human exercises, for example, overfishing and waterfront improvement. GIS apparatuses help in the plan of marine safeguarded regions, the evaluation of marine biodiversity, and the preparation of protection techniques to save delicate marine environments.

Difficulties and Future Headings:

While GIS and remote detecting have become necessary to preservation, a few difficulties and contemplations continue:

Information Quality and Openness:

The adequacy of GIS and remote detecting applications depends on the accessibility and nature of spatial information. Guaranteeing admittance to high-goal and modern information, particularly in remote or information scant districts, stays a test.

Limit Building and Preparing:

Protectionists and experts need the abilities to tackle the maximum capacity of GIS and remote detecting advancements. Limit building programs are fundamental to engage people and associations with the information and aptitude to utilize these devices actually.

Interdisciplinary Joint effort:

Protection challenges are many times complex and require interdisciplinary methodologies. Cooperation between traditionalists, geographers, biologists, and information researchers is pivotal to creating thorough arrangements that coordinate spatial data with environmental bits of knowledge.

Moral Contemplations:

The utilization of GIS and remote detecting raises moral contemplations, including issues of security, information proprietorship, and the possible abuse of innovation. Creating moral rules and guidelines for the capable utilization of spatial information is fundamental.

Joining with Native Information:

Coordinating native information and conventional environmental insight with GIS applications is basic for thinking up all encompassing protection methodologies. Regard for neighborhood points of view upgrades the viability and social significance of preservation endeavors.

Headways in Innovation:

The field of GIS and remote detecting is dynamic, with nonstop progressions in innovation. Keeping up to date with new devices, sensors, and logical techniques guarantees that moderates can use the furthest down the line advancements to address arising difficulties.

Future Headings:

Open Information Stages and Coordinated effort:

Advancing open information stages and cooperative drives improves information sharing, straightforwardness, and the aggregate effect of GIS and remote detecting applications. Open-source devices and stages add to the democratization of spatial information, permitting a more extensive local area to take part in preservation endeavors.

Man-made consciousness and AI Combination:

The combination of man-made brainpower (simulated intelligence) and AI (ML) upgrades the abilities of GIS in information examination and translation. Computer based intelligence calculations can mechanize the handling of enormous datasets, distinguish designs, and add to additional precise expectations and groupings.

Constant Observing and Sensor Organizations:

Propels in sensor advancements and availability empower constant observing through organizations of sensors. Conveying sensor networks in basic territories gives ceaseless information streams, offering dynamic experiences into natural circumstances and empowering fast reactions to arising dangers.

Resident Science and Local area Commitment:

Connecting with residents in information assortment and checking through resident science drives improves the spatial information accessible for preservation. Local area cooperation encourages a feeling of pride and obligation regarding nearby conditions, adding to the progress of preservation programs.

Advancement in Remote Detecting Advances:

Proceeded with advancement in remote detecting advances, including the improvement of little satellites, hyperspectral sensors, and high level imaging strategies, upgrades the accuracy and variety of information that can be caught. These developments grow the scope of utilizations for preservation.

6.3 Collaborative efforts between researchers, NGOs, and governments

Cooperative endeavors between specialists, non-legislative associations (NGOs), and state run administrations are crucial in tending to complex worldwide difficulties. By pooling mastery, assets, and viewpoints, these associations cultivate creative answers for issues going from biodiversity preservation to general wellbeing. Specialists contribute state of the art information, NGOs bring grassroots commitment and backing, while legislatures give strategy structures and administrative help. This cooperative collaboration guarantees a complete and maintainable way to deal with handling major problems, advancing a common obligation regarding the prosperity of our planet and its occupants.

CHAPTER 7

Community Involvement And Education

Preservation endeavors are at their best when they effectively include and engage nearby networks. The cooperative energy between preservation drives and the commitment of networks is a strong power that safeguards biodiversity as well as advances manageable turn of events. This investigation digs into the basic job of local area contribution and schooling in preservation, analyzing effective models, challenges, and the groundbreaking effect of cultivating natural stewardship inside networks.

**1. The Nexus Among Protection and Networks:

The association between solid environments and the prosperity of neighborhood networks is evident. For protection to be maintainable, it should address the necessities and goals of those living in nearness to basic natural surroundings. Perceiving this, numerous protection projects presently focus on local area inclusion as a principal part of their methodologies.

**2. Examples of overcoming adversity in Local area Based Preservation:

1. The Instance of Namibian People group Conservancies:
   Namibia's People group Based Regular Asset The executives (CB-NRM) program remains as a guide of progress in local area based protection. Through the foundation of conservancies, neighborhood networks gain possession and the board freedoms over untamed life and normal assets. This model has not just added to the recuperation of imperiled species like the dark rhinoceros yet has additionally enabled networks financially through supportable the travel industry and prize hunting income.
2. Local area Timberland The executives in Nepal:

Nepal's People group Woodland The executives represents a fruitful local area driven protection approach. By giving nearby networks command over assigned woods regions, this drive has eased back deforestation as well as upgraded jobs through manageable asset use. The strengthening of networks as stewards of their timberlands has brought about superior biodiversity protection and local area versatility.

**3. Challenges in Local area Commitment:

While the advantages of local area contribution in protection are apparent, challenges continue. These difficulties include:

1. Restricted Assets:
   Numerous neighborhood networks miss the mark on monetary and specialized assets expected to take part in preservation endeavors effectively. Inadequate subsidizing and limit building open doors can thwart local area commitment.
2. Clashing Interests:
   Adjusting preservation objectives with the financial necessities of networks can be complicated. Clashes might emerge when protection estimates influence customary jobs, prompting obstruction or resistance.
3. Absence of Instruction and Mindfulness:

Now and again, networks may not completely comprehend the significance of preservation or the drawn out benefits it can bring. Training and mindfulness programs are significant for encouraging a feeling of ecological stewardship.

**4. The Groundbreaking Force of Schooling:

Training fills in as an impetus for changing networks into dynamic members in preservation. At the point when networks are furnished with information about their nearby environments, the worth of biodiversity, and maintainable practices, they become educated advocates for preservation. Instructive drives can take different structures:

1. School Projects:
   Coordinating ecological training into school educational plans imparts a preservation ethic in the more youthful age. Schools become centers for advancing mindfulness about neighborhood biological systems and the interconnectedness between human exercises and the climate.
2. Local area Studios and Preparing:
   Directing studios and instructional meetings for local area individuals

improves how they might interpret preservation standards and practices. These meetings can cover subjects like practical agribusiness, living space reclamation, and natural life observing.

3. Data Missions:

Sending off data crusades utilizing different media channels scatters information about the significance of biodiversity protection. Public help declarations, radio projects, and local area occasions add to building mindfulness.

5. Enabling Ladies in Preservation:
Perceiving the essential job ladies play in local area elements and maintainable turn of events, preservation drives progressively center around engaging ladies. At the point when ladies are effectively associated with dynamic cycles and get to instruction and assets, the effect on preservation is significant. The foundation of ladies drove preservation gatherings, as found in projects like the Maijuna Native Ladies' Relationship in the Peruvian Amazon, shows the way that ladies can be strong problem solvers in local area based protection.

6. Native Information and Protection:
Native people group frequently have customary information that is important for preservation. Their profound comprehension of neighborhood biological systems, maintainable asset the board practices, and conjunction with untamed life can altogether add to protection endeavors. Perceiving and regarding native information frameworks encourages a cooperative methodology that adjusts protection objectives to the insight gathered over ages.

7. Monetary Motivators for Protection:
Connecting protection endeavors with monetary motivators for networks is an essential methodology. Feasible the travel industry, installment for biological system administrations, and fair-exchange accreditation for harmless to the ecosystem items are instances of monetary models that benefit both preservation objectives and local area prosperity. By exhibiting the monetary worth of protection, networks are bound to partake in and support preservation drives effectively.

8. The Job of Innovation in Local area Commitment:
Innovation can assume an extraordinary part in local area commitment for preservation. Versatile applications for resident science, remote detecting apparatuses for observing, and online instructive assets expand the extent of local area association. These mechanical headways span holes in correspondence, improve information assortment, and enable networks with continuous data.

9. Associations Between NGOs, States, and Networks:

Fruitful people group based protection frequently includes associations between non-legislative associations (NGOs), states, and neighborhood networks.

NGOs can bring specialized aptitude, financing, and venture the executives abilities, while states offer administrative help and foundation. Local area contribution guarantees that protection drives line up with neighborhood needs and social settings.

10. Contextual analysis: The Gobi Bear Preservation Venture:

The Gobi bear, an uncommon and imperiled animal varieties possessing the Gobi Desert in Mongolia, is the focal point of a cooperative preservation exertion. The Gobi Bear Preservation Undertaking includes nearby networks, NGOs, and the Mongolian government cooperating to safeguard the environment of this slippery bear. Through people group commitment, instructive projects, and reasonable advancement drives, the venture points not exclusively to protect the Gobi bear yet additionally to work on the occupations of those living in the district.

7.1 Engaging local communities in tiger conservation

Tiger protection isn't exclusively the obligation of traditionalists and administrative bodies; it requires the dynamic cooperation and backing of neighborhood networks dwelling in and around tiger territories. Connecting with nearby networks in tiger preservation drives is vital for the outcome of these endeavors. This investigation dives into the multi-layered parts of local area commitment, featuring effective models, challenges confronted, and the groundbreaking effect of encouraging a feeling of responsibility and stewardship among those living in closeness to these notable huge felines.

1. The Significance of Local area Commitment:

1. Shared Living spaces and Shared Liabilities:
   Tigers frequently coincide with human populaces, sharing scenes that are indispensable for both the endurance of the species and the jobs of nearby networks. Drawing in these networks is fundamental as their day to day exercises, land use examples, and collaborations with untamed life straightforwardly impact the preservation status of tigers.
2. Grasping Nearby Viewpoints:

Neighborhood people group have extraordinary experiences into the biological elements of their environmental factors. Grasping their viewpoints, customary information, and concerns is vital for making preservation techniques that are compelling and socially touchy.

**2. Effective Models of Local area Commitment:

1. Local area Oversaw Stores:
   Laying out local area oversaw saves has demonstrated effective in nations like Nepal and India. By giving nearby networks freedoms over regular assets and including them in dynamic cycles, these stores become safe houses for untamed life as well as wellsprings of feasible jobs.
2. Eco-The travel industry and Practical Jobs:

Coordinating eco-the travel industry drives into tiger protection plans makes financial motivations for neighborhood networks to effectively take part in defending these superb felines. Effective models can be found in districts like the Sundarbans in Bangladesh, where local area based eco-the travel industry upholds both protection and work improvement.

**3. Challenges in Local area Commitment:

1. Human-Natural life Struggle:
   The nearness of human settlements to tiger territories can prompt contentions, with tigers going after domesticated animals or incidentally presenting dangers to human wellbeing. Tending to these contentions requires imaginative arrangements that balance the necessities of networks and the protection of tigers.
2. Neediness and Criminal operations:
   Neediness can drive networks to take part in criminal operations, like poaching and living space annihilation, to meet their fundamental necessities. Successful people group commitment includes tending to fundamental financial issues and giving other option, feasible work choices.
3. Absence of Mindfulness and Schooling:

At times, neighborhood networks might need mindfulness about the significance of tiger protection and the job they can play. Instruction and mindfulness programs are imperative for encouraging a feeling of obligation and natural stewardship.

**4. Instruction and Mindfulness Projects:

1. School Drives:
   Coordinating tiger preservation into school educational plans imparts

a feeling of obligation in the more youthful age. Instructive projects can incorporate data about tiger biology, the significance of biodiversity, and the job of networks in protection.

2. Local area Studios and Preparing:

Leading studios and instructional meetings for local area individuals improves how they might interpret preservation standards and practices. These meetings can cover points like conjunction systems, announcing untamed life sightings, and the financial advantages of protection.

**5. Financial Motivators and Supportable Vocations:

1. Local area Based Preservation Ventures:
   Laying out local area based preservation ventures gives nearby networks financial motivations to take part in tiger protection effectively. This could incorporate the advancement of feasible organizations, for example, handiworks, directed untamed life visits, or eco-accommodating horticulture.
2. Installment for Environment Administrations:

Investigating installment for environment administrations (PES) models, where networks get pay for keeping up with sound biological systems, can be an incredible asset. This perceives the job networks play in saving basic territories for tigers.

**6. Contextual analyses in Local area Commitment:

1. Bardiya Public Park, Nepal:
   In Bardiya Public Park, Nepal, the Cradle Zone The board Advisory group engages neighborhood networks by including them in dynamic cycles. The panel directs local area oversaw ventures, for example, feasible the travel industry, guaranteeing that monetary advantages stream back to those effectively taken part in protection.
2. Periyar Tiger Save, India:

Periyar Tiger Save in India is eminent for its effective local area based protection model. Neighborhood people group are effectively engaged with watching, checking, and dealing with the hold. Moreover, income produced from eco-the travel industry upholds local area improvement projects, making an immediate connection between tiger protection and neighborhood prosperity.

**7. Tending to Human-Natural life Struggle:

1. Early Admonition Frameworks:
   Carrying out early advance notice frameworks that ready networks about the presence of tigers in the area can assist with diminishing struggles. This permits networks to go to preventive lengths, shield domesticated animals, and keep away from conflicts with these dominant hunters.
2. Animals Protection Projects:

Presenting animals protection projects can give pay to networks to misfortunes caused because of tiger predation. This mitigates the monetary effect of struggles, lessening the probability of retaliatory measures against tigers.

**8. Social Awareness and Native Information:

Perceiving and regarding nearby societies and native information frameworks is essential to effective local area commitment. Native people group frequently have customary practices that advance conjunction with untamed life. Integrating this information into protection plans encourages a cooperative methodology and upgrades the viability of drives.

**9. Innovation for Local area Commitment:

1. Versatile Applications for Announcing:
   Creating versatile applications that empower networks to report tiger sightings, poaching exercises, or potential contentions upgrades correspondence and information assortment. These applications work with ongoing data dividing among networks and preservation specialists.
2. Advanced Training Stages:

Utilizing computerized stages for instruction and mindfulness crusades empowers the dispersal of data to a more extensive crowd. Online assets, recordings, and intuitive substance can arrive at networks even in distant regions.

**10. Local area Strengthening through Ladies' Inclusion:

Engaging ladies inside neighborhood networks is an essential methodology. Ladies frequently assume vital parts in regular asset the executives and local area elements. Drives that include and engage ladies add to more all encompassing and manageable protection results.

**11. The Job of NGOs and Government Backing:

1. NGO Organizations:
   Joint efforts between non-legislative associations (NGOs) and

neighborhood networks are instrumental in carrying out effective preservation drives. NGOs can give specialized mastery, financing, and venture the board support, while networks contribute neighborhood information and labor.

2. Government Backing:

Legislatures assume a crucial part in making strategies that help local area commitment in tiger protection. Perceiving and formalizing the freedoms of nearby networks over normal assets and including them in dynamic cycles add to the progress of preservation endeavors.

12. Checking and Versatile Administration:

Normal checking of local area commitment drives considers versatile administration. Surveying the effect of preservation systems, gathering input from networks, and making changes in view of advancing conditions guarantee the viability and maintainability of these endeavors.

7.2 Educational programs to raise awareness about habitat fragmentation

Environment discontinuity represents a huge danger to biodiversity, upsetting biological systems and imperiling the endurance of incalculable species. Teaching the general population about the results of territory fracture is urgent for cultivating mindfulness, empowering capable way of behaving, and collecting support for preservation endeavors. This investigation dives into the significance of instructive projects zeroed in on environment fracture, looking at key systems, effective drives, and the extraordinary effect of informed networks on the way to biological maintainability.

1. Figuring out the Effect of Living space Fracture:

Instructive projects assume a critical part in assisting people with getting a handle on the complexities and results of environment fracture. Understanding that this interaction includes the separating of once consistent living spaces into more modest, disconnected patches is essential. These projects dig into the environmental consequences, accentuating how discontinuity hinders species development, upsets normal cycles, and prompts biodiversity misfortune.

2. Focusing on Assorted Crowds:

Instructive drives should take special care of different crowds, going from schoolchildren to grown-ups, to guarantee an inescapable comprehension of living space fracture. Fitting substance to various age gatherings, instructive levels, and local area settings upgrades the adequacy of these projects. For schools, coordinating illustrations on living space fracture into educational plans gives an establishment to ecological stewardship since early on.

**3. Intelligent Learning:

Connecting with, intuitive growth opportunities catch consideration and leave an enduring effect. Integrating field outings, studios, and involved exercises permits members to observe the impacts of environment discontinuity firsthand. Nature strolls, untamed life following, and intelligent reenactments extend the comprehension of the intricacies encompassing divided scenes.

**4. Using Advanced Stages:

In the computerized age, online stages give a strong medium to instructive effort. Using sites, web-based entertainment, and instructive applications considers the scattering of data to a more extensive crowd. Virtual visits, intelligent guides, and media introductions upgrade the openness and commitment of instructive substance on territory fracture.

**5. Coordinated effort with Schools and Establishments:

Framing organizations with instructive establishments, like schools and colleges, is instrumental in carrying out successful instructive projects. Incorporating living space discontinuity points into existing science and ecological examinations educational plans guarantees that understudies get organized and far reaching instruction regarding the matter.

**6. Connecting with Local area Pioneers and Powerhouses:

Local area pioneers and forces to be reckoned with use huge impact in forming popular assessment. Working together with nearby pioneers, natural activists, and powerhouses can intensify the compass of instructive projects. Public discussions, local area studios, and mindfulness crusades drove by regarded figures assist with conveying the desperation of tending to natural surroundings discontinuity.

**7. Contextual analyses and Genuine Models:

Consolidating contextual investigations and genuine models grandstands the unmistakable effect of living space fracture on unambiguous species and biological systems. Featuring examples of overcoming adversity where protection estimates switched discontinuity related difficulties gives trust and exhibits the viability of informed activity.

**8. Tending to Human-Natural life Struggle:

Instructive projects should resolve the mind boggling issue of human-natural life struggle, frequently exacerbated by living space fracture. Assisting people group with figuring out the interconnectedness of biological systems, the job of natural life passages, and the significance of conjunction cultivates sympathy and advances arrangements that benefit the two people and untamed life.

9. Advancing Supportable Land Use Practices:
Training about environment fracture remains closely connected with advancing manageable land use rehearses. Empowering dependable turn of events, pushing for untamed life well disposed foundation, and accentuating the significance of keeping up with environmental availability are key parts of these projects.

10. Estimating Effect and Adjusting Techniques:
Surveying the effect of instructive projects is critical for refining systems and guaranteeing continuous viability. Reviews, criticism meetings, and observing changes in local area conduct and perspectives give important bits of knowledge. Versatile administration permits coordinators to tailor future drives in view of the developing necessities and comprehension of the interest group.

11. Public-Private Associations:
Coordinated effort among public and confidential elements upgrades the span and assets accessible for instructive projects. Confidential organizations, especially those with a huge effect ashore use, can add to bringing issues to light about natural surroundings fracture and partake in preservation drives.

12. Advancing Resident Science:
Engaging residents to add to logical endeavors through resident science projects adds a viable aspect to instructive projects. Including people group in information assortment, observing neighborhood natural life, and adding to explore projects imparts a feeling of pride and obligation.

13. Worldwide Joint effort and Data Trade:
Considering that natural surroundings discontinuity is a worldwide issue, it is fundamental for cultivate global joint effort. Instructive projects ought to stress the interconnectedness of biological systems around the world, empowering a feeling of worldwide obligation and the sharing of effective protection techniques.

14. Promotion and Strategy Mindfulness:
Instructive drives shouldn't just illuminate yet in addition enable people to advocate for strategy changes that address natural surroundings fracture. Bringing issues to light about the job of strategies in alleviating discontinuity and empowering public support in approach conversations add to fundamental change.

15. Assessing Long haul Conduct Change:
A definitive objective of instructive projects is to incite long haul conduct change. Assessing whether members embrace feasible practices, support preservation endeavors, and effectively take part in natural surroundings security drives measures the outcome of these projects.

7.3 Empowering communities to become stewards of tiger habitats

Engaging nearby networks to become stewards of tiger territories is an extraordinary methodology that not just guarantees the prosperity of these glorious large felines yet additionally encourages supportable concurrence among people and natural life. This strengthening includes giving networks the information, assets, and motivations expected to partake in the preservation and assurance of tiger territories effectively. By making a feeling of pride and obligation, this approach turns into a strong impetus for the protection of both biodiversity and the livelihoods of those living in nearness to these notorious species.

1. Building Ecological Mindfulness:

The most vital phase in engaging networks is to assemble natural mindfulness. Local area individuals need to comprehend the significance of tiger living spaces in keeping up with natural equilibrium and supporting biodiversity. Instructive projects, studios, and mindfulness missions can convey the meaning of sound environments, stressing the job of tigers as dominant hunters and marks of biological system wellbeing.

2. Sharing Conventional Information:

Nearby people group frequently have conventional information about their environmental elements, including experiences into the way of behaving and nature of tigers. Perceiving and regarding this native information is critical for fruitful protection. By making stages for the trading of conventional insight and logical mastery, networks can effectively add to the comprehension and insurance of tiger environments.

3. Local area Based Protection Arranging:

Strengthening includes giving networks a voice in protection arranging. Drawing in local area individuals in the improvement of protection procedures guarantees that these plans line up with nearby necessities and real factors. Cooperative dynamic cycles upgrade the feeling of responsibility, making networks more put resources into the progress of preservation drives.

4. Financial Motivations for Protection:

Connecting preservation endeavors with financial motivating forces is an essential method for enabling networks. Reasonable job choices, for example, eco-the travel industry, local area based endeavors, and capable regular asset the executives, give monetary advantages to networks effectively engaged with tiger environment preservation. This approach shows the way that the conservation of biological systems can add to worked on financial prosperity.

5. Limit Building Drives:

Strengthening requires building the limit of networks to participate in environment stewardship effectively. Preparing programs on natural life checking, environment reclamation, and supportable farming practices furnish local area individuals with the abilities expected to contribute actually to preservation endeavors. These drives upgrade the capacity of networks to go with informed choices and go to proactive lengths for environment insurance.

**6. Natural life agreeable Land Use Practices:

Empowering untamed life amicable land use rehearses is fundamental for cultivating conjunction. Enabled people group are bound to take on rehearses that diminish human-untamed life struggle, like the foundation of cradle zones, capable garbage removal, and the utilization of non-deadly impediments to safeguard domesticated animals. These practices establish conditions where tigers can flourish without representing a danger to local area vocations.

**7. Laying out Natural life Hallways:

Strengthening includes working cooperatively to lay out and keep up with natural life hallways. These fundamental associations between divided living spaces empower tigers and other natural life to move openly, advancing hereditary variety and generally speaking biological system wellbeing. Drawing in networks in the recognizable proof and assurance of these passageways supports the interconnectedness of natural surroundings and the significance of scene level preservation.

**8. Local area Drove Hostile to Poaching Drives:

Engaged people group are pivotal partners in the battle against poaching. Preparing people group individuals as natural life watchmen, laying out local area based enemy of poaching units, and carrying out careful observing frameworks make a cutting edge protection against criminal operations. Strengthening imparts a feeling of obligation, transforming networks into dynamic defenders of tiger populaces.

**9. Tending to Human-Untamed life Struggle:

Strengthening includes outfitting networks with systems to address human-natural life struggle. Early admonition frameworks, local area drove reaction groups, and the execution of compelling animals security measures add to limiting contentions. By furnishing networks with the devices to coincide calmly with untamed life, strengthening turns into a useful answer for decreasing negative connections.

**10. Advancing Practical Horticulture:

Empowering reasonable horticultural practices is necessary to natural surroundings stewardship. Enabled people group can embrace agroecological approaches that limit environment aggravation, diminish substance inputs, and advance biodiversity in farming scenes. This combination of preservation and maintainable agribusiness lines up with the more extensive objective of encouraging amicability between human exercises and tiger living spaces.

**11. Public-Private Associations:

Cooperation between nearby networks and confidential substances, like protection associations and organizations, enhances the effect of strengthening drives. Public-private organizations can bring extra assets, mastery, and amazing open doors for local area drove projects. These joint efforts reinforce the limit of networks to partake in environment stewardship effectively.

**12. Perceiving Ladies as Protection Pioneers:

Strengthening ought to perceive the imperative job ladies play in protection. Drawing in and enabling ladies inside networks upgrades the adequacy of preservation drives. Ladies frequently go about as essential guardians, teachers, and chiefs in asset the board. Perceiving and supporting their administration adds to all encompassing and reasonable environment stewardship.

**13. Observing and Variation:

Strengthening is a continuous interaction that requires checking and variation. Normal appraisals of the effect of strengthening drives, input from networks, and the adaptability to adjust procedures in light of changing conditions guarantee the supported viability of these projects.

**14. Observing Achievement and Local area Champions:

Perceiving and commending examples of overcoming adversity inside enabled networks is fundamental. Local area champions who effectively add to environment stewardship ought to be recognized and celebrated. This uplifting feedback supports a culture of stewardship and moves others to play a functioning job in preservation.

www.ingramcontent.com/pod-product-compliance
Lightning Source LLC
LaVergne TN
LVHW010646200726
843507LV00011B/1767